Published by Ricochet Editions
http://ricocheteditions.com

ricochet

Ricochet titles are distributed by Small Press Distribution
www.spdbooks.org / 800-869-7553

This title is also available for purchase directly from the publisher

Library of Congress Cataloging-in-Publication Data
Holiday, Harmony
Go Find Your Father | A Famous Blues / Harmony Holiday
Library of Congress Control Number 2013947658

ISBN 9781938900082

9 8 7 6 5 4 3 2 1

FIRST EDITION

GO FIND YOUR FATHER

HARMONY HOLIDAY

SONG TITLE	ASSOCIATED PARTIES
IF I CAN'T CHANGE THE WORLD DON...	WRI:HOLIDAY, JIMMY
	PUB:JOBETE MUSIC CO INC
	OLD BROMPTON ROAD MUSIC
	ABC MUSIC
IT'S GOOD TO BE HOME	WRI:HOLIDAY, JIMMY
	HOLIDAY, ELIZABETH
	PUB:JOBETE MUSIC CO INC
	OLD BROMPTON ROAD MUSIC
JIMMY CARTER	WRI:HOLIDAY, JIMMY
	WOODS, MARCIA
	PUB:JOBETE MUSIC CO INC
	OLD BROMPTON ROAD MUSIC
JUST MAKE IT SIMPLE	WRI:HOLIDAY, JIMMY
	PACKARD, JACKIE
	PUB:JOBETE MUSIC CO INC
	OLD BROMPTON ROAD MUSIC
	ABC MUSIC
KEEP ON TALKIN'	WRI:HOLIDAY, JIMMY
	HOLIDAY, ELIZABETH
	PUB:JOBETE MUSIC CO INC
	OLD BROMPTON ROAD MUSIC
LET NO ONE CATCH YOU CRYING	WRI:HOLIDAY, JIMMY
	PUB:JOBETE MUSIC CO INC
	OLD BROMPTON ROAD MUSIC
LISTEN TO MY STORY	WRI:HOLIDAY, JIMMY
	WOODS, MARCIA
	PUB:JOBETE MUSIC CO INC
	OLD BROMPTON ROAD MUSIC
LIVE TO RUN AGAIN	WRI:HOLIDAY, JIMMY
	AULDIN, NANCY
	PUB:JOBETE MUSIC CO INC
	OLD BROMPTON ROAD MUSIC
LOVE AND LAW	WRI:HOLIDAY, JIMMY
	ROGERS, LEE
	PUB:JOBETE MUSIC CO INC
	OLD BROMPTON ROAD MUSIC
	ABC MUSIC
LOVE IS A GIFT	WRI:HOLIDAY, JIMMY
	PUB:JOBETE MUSIC CO INC
	OLD BROMPTON ROAD MUSIC
LOVE WON'T LIVE HERE (SINCE YO...	WRI:HOLIDAY, JIMMY
	BOMAN FRANK
	PUB:JOBETE MUSIC CO INC
	OLD BROMPTON ROAD MUSIC

SONG TITLE	ASSOCIATED PARTIES
	PUB: JOBETE MUSIC CO I
	OLD BROMPTON ROAD
STAY WITH ME	WRI: HOLIDAY, JIMMY
	PUB: JOBETE MUSIC CO I
	OLD BROMPTON ROAD
STOP	WRI: HOLIDAY, JIMMY
	PUB: JOBETE MUSIC CO I
	OLD BROMPTON ROAD
THE BIG TOWN	WRI: HOLIDAY, JIMMY
	HOLIDAY, ELIZABET
	PUB: JOBETE MUSIC CO I
	OLD BROMPTON ROAD
THE BOOK OF MY LIFE	WRI: HOLIDAY, JIMMY
	WOODS, MARCIA

I'm one of your children, actually. I was one of your children. You got a bunch of children, man... you got a bunch of children, brother. I still am. Will be. For instance, I will never take no shit, your legacy. I will never believe anybody can tell me shit unless they are something I can feel— something I can feel.

THE WORLD WE LIVE IN	WRI: HOLIDAY, JIMMY
	PUB: JOBETE MUSIC CO I
	OLD BROMPTON ROAD

— AMIRI BARAKA, *OBITUARY FOR MILES DAVIS*

	WRI: HOLIDAY, JIMMY
	PUB: JOBETE MUSIC CO I
	OLD BROMPTON ROAD
	ABC MUSIC
WEEP FOR THEM (WEEP FOR ME)	WRI: HOLIDAY, JIMMY
	KING, LEE ANN
	PUB: JOBETE MUSIC CO I
	OLD BROMPTON ROAD
	ABC MUSIC
WHEN I'M LOVING YOU	WRI: HOLIDAY, JIMMY
	MARIE-JONNE
	SWITZLER, PAUL
	PUB: JOBETE MUSIC CO I
	OLD BROMPTON ROAD
	ABC MUSIC
WORRIED	WRI: HOLIDAY, JIMMY
	PUB: JOBETE MUSIC CO I
	OLD BROMPTON ROAD
	ABC MUSIC
YOU'RE GETTING BETTER	WRI: HOLIDAY, JIMMY
	ROGERS, LEE

ENTIETH CENTURY ROCK N RO		50-015581-7	W	TOWNSEND ED
			P	DAMIE MUSIC INC
DERSTANDING IS THE BEST T		51-001610-9	W	HOLIDAY JAMES E
			W	CHARLES RAY
			P	METRIC MUSIC CO
ARE THE FUTURE		53-023373-9	W	LAWS TROY
			W	WOMACK FRIENDLY
			W	BOLTON MELTON
			W	HOLIDAY JAMES E
			P	OLD BROMPTON ROAD
			P	DERGLENN MUSIC
GOT A GOOD THING GOIN		53-014799-4	W	HOLIDAY JAMES E
			P	METRIC MUSIC CO
ERE SHE AT		53-014702-9	W	HOLIDAY JAMES E
			W	LEWIS JIMMY
			W	CHAMBERS CLIFFORD
			P	METRIC MUSIC CO
Y DID SHE LEAVE ME		53-018266-0	W	HOLIDAY JAMES E
			W	FLOYD KING
			P	HOUSE OF JOSEPH
S MY GOODNESS YES		55-006497-4	W	BUTLER JERRY
			W	HOLIDAY JAMES E
			W	WOMACK BOBBY
			P	PARABUT MUS CORP
			P	TRACEBOB MUSIC
STERDAY DIED	(F)	55-009740-2	W	DE SHANNON JACKIE
			W	HOLIDAY JAMES E
			W	MYERS RANDY JAMES
			P	UNITED ARTISTS MUSIC CO
			P	UNART MUSIC CORP
U GOT TO SHARE		55-005970-2	W	HOLIDAY JAMES E
			W	LEWIS JIMMY
			W	CHAMBER CLIFFORD
			P	METRIC MUSIC CO

TAL NUMBER OF SONGS...... 60

DEAR DAD,

I had another dream about you last night. A chant running through it: *Today is the day that you give your heart to Jesus, today is the day that you give your life to Allah, today is the day that give your heart to Ra, today is the day that you give your mind Osiris, today is the day that you give your heart to Shiva Horus, today is the day that you give your heart to Jesus, today is the day that you give your heart to Jah, today is the day, today is*—the preacher kept going, so syncretic and assured, such synchrony and its cronies: allure, allure, allegory, sure-shot, he spoke the rock up and down the hillside, deity after deity or god after god. You were there with him in one of those small black churches in your hometown of Sallis, Mississippi: Stetson hat, slacks, crisp track shirt, and cowboy boots to his three-piece suit. And you just peered at the preacher for a while, gaze shot with a mixture of dismissal and rapture the way Tony Williams appears when he plays the drums with his *Lifetime Experience* band, especially on the song **I Love You More Than What's Happening**—and then you got up and walked out like a G, like a true believer.

Next thing I knew you were running like triumph and inverse fugitive, slow and shirtless through a gorgeous flaxen cotton/field-negro-glamour, arms outstretched, looking glad and regal and I was on the other side of time, way across that field, playing Monk's *Ask Me Now* on a burning piano, improvising with the flames so literally we became abstract for a moment, legends acting out our inter-dimensional destinies with ecstatic obedience. And we both seemed wild-calm from it, and intent, like dancers rehearsing choreography for a grand performance of a future that is the past for us, but that remains a future, like mythocrats, we were/I want to say *are*. And it seemed like we were aware that standing still brought us closer than any gesture toward one another and like that was part of our routine, how we kept gesturing anyways, in the interest of intervals and rhythms, you with the running, me with the fire music. *Today is the day...ask me now...today is that the day that you give your he(art) to...ask me now*—and I woke up with the lyrics to *I Love You More Than What's Happening* so vivid in my head:

There comes a time to wake up to what's happening,
There comes a time to get out of what's happening,
I love you more than what's happening.

Happier than the morning sun, your daughter,
Harmony

I seen it happen, I scene/it happen/I see it all/ways

ALTERNATE ENDING / WHY WE ARE A DESTINY / WHY ARE WE A DESTINY

Saturn, we learn, devours his children, afraid that otherwise they will surpass him. One is born who escapes with the help of the mother, and the cycle breaks, so the myth informs us like a quiet uncle with wise tendencies. That's all he'll tell us and then he goes back to gazing off into the distance as the lull of the party upsurges around him. You think he's drunk but he's just thinking with a myth keeping the cool in his palm. The smell of bbq and ambivalence. Stereotype, lifestyle, still life with don't move or I'll shoot. A blues parallel, a crop circle, a rhinestone sharecropper, a yellow girl enters the red wheelbarrow and the chicken gotta go. And sacrifice is an acoustic condition, we learn, so much of it depends upon the way the drums pick up and snag just when you're about to heave into the body of an animal and release the blood from the spirit, the rhythm gets so close to disapproval that it feels like permission, or at least good excuse, and even if you aren't there, you know it when it happens. That's the birth of the search.

I'm talking about the moment you first felt the trapdoor leading from disappearance to loss, bolted with the energy of the rhythm of your **heartbeat/he-art-be-at/titude/realdeal**. You're pounding on the door and you can feel
it expand and clamp around you like a so-what tornado because of the very weight of your need to see inside its all-enveloping eye. Out of the velocity of your willed opening an enclosure is tendered, that's our love for the father, or for the blood of ourselves   and we know   **The blood of the thing is the truth of the thing.** I'm talking about the

last time you saw your father.

How you're suddenly in the Mississippi/Delta and the river floods with skyscrapers
and Rolls Royce limousines and brass instruments and the rusty tracks of defunct
train lines and the fat asses of extinct buffalo and corroded race records with groups of black men
and women huddled on the covers looking like tribes and disking down the water like mutant
pirates, or monuments gulped out of recorded history through treble and bleed—and all these objects
haul an hallucination
through all your mind, and you begin to understand what Malcolm X's archivist meant when he
said, *This country doesn't allow black men to mature. It allows them to grow up, physically. But it doesn't allow them to mature,*
mentally, emotionally, and spiritually.

You begin to see the objects in this river acid trip as objects in your father's mind jetting through
hindsight like screeching breaks every time he goes to speak; you begin to see that drugged river as
the subject of Black Music of *Blues People*—from when blue was our favorite color. You hear Langston's
euphoric/anaphoric *I've Known Rivers* differently; you hear it as the moment of trance
and lucid self-awareness made bearable by rhythm. Just when his heart can
handle the beating of all that capital against its natural running/water, that child is born and he
disappears just as clean and pivotal as a sanctuary—All you're left with is that memory of him staring
at the river and singing about a war within (as in his own words, so in his own wars), and with that
we'll trace ourselves from the black gods to the black divas to black collectivity and back, finding
(that) our blood runs as and of that river.

I want to talk about the relationship between black men and women and our fathers, as I understand it. This means I want to discuss growing up black/brown/yellow/gold-in America and not knowing your own father or being afraid of him or forcing naiveté in order to understand him or taking him for granted because you landed in a fairy tale and didn't know he was the author like in *Those Winter Sundays*, or him being one form or another of gone: Iron Mask or Cosby Sweater or Nowhere Man, I want to talk about that. And I want to talk about how that moody, pageanting oracle affects and defects the main arteries running through the whole nation: how when black men are both revered and feared from the inside out by their children as much as by their nation as much as by themselves, how the country becomes a playground for **the triptych so-trite fantasy, at once folk hero and folk villain and the rituals and ceremonies therein**. How my imagination **grabs that baton on my leg/Legba**, of the relay/race, and dashes with it. I want to talk about how reclaiming the power of myth in the name of the father might undo some of the delusions of the so-called Black Aesthetic Tradition, may let us into our radical (coming from the root) inventions, not as desperate trespassers but as fearless healers no longer afraid of a correspondence between disappearance and loss, or between the seen and the unseen; aware again, long-keen and kin again, that *Every Goodbye Ain't Gone.*

He still be screamin', he still be screamin', I see his demons in empty hallways

DEAR DAD,

That time you were cleaning your gun and forgot that it was loaded; shot a bullet right through your left fuck-you finger, got it sewn back together, got your sound back together, what a beautiful flying saucer across our living room, what a talking book. No judgment whatsoever. Actually I think every black male soul singer in the federation has to pawn love for 45s once-in-a-while, the Mississippi millimeter, the width between the me and the scene on the map made *Ma'at*, not that that's what it was, the swell of blood around our verses, versus the blood on the leaves, blood at the roots, where it gets tough, and tuff too, but you were, and are, our true wooden soldier; we wouldn't have sold that blast, that day, for the whole wide/white world, and the wound of it bloomed like longing flowers, longing to bleed for their beauty. *Swoon, swoon, swoon, win me back.* I don't remember the sound it made, I just recall the white cloth on black metal caped like magic and arose as compass, cupid arrows, so-what bliss. And that we knew you were not afraid and grew fearless with you. Catharsis, arson, total sanity overcame us like a weakness for stories. *Didn't wanna have to do it, didn't wanna have to do it.* Even now. Odd future. You do write, and we do write. Listening to Prog Rock, listening to you sing and watch, listening to the night close like a trapdoor as that vast calm makes us wish we'd been dreaming.

Fearlessly and with love,
Harmony

DEAR DAD,

I'm trying something new. I'm proud of myself this time too. I have to twist my cheek to one side to keep from crying, though maybe the tears are a skin I need to shed. A skin faster than words. It's early summer. The living is easy, my pa's rich and my mother's good looking. Close enough. Songs come true. Gershwin's stolen folk hero or folk villain, returning, returning. A few years back I was set on rewriting *Porgy and Bess*, adapting it, distracting it from its own xenophobia with the grace of re-appropriation. I think I'm the perfect person for that task. First of all who else would even want to attempt that, second of all, being both black and white in the blood, if you believe in that kind of thing, I understand the pimps as well as the hoes, the desperate and the despotic. Dad, you really helped to create a prime/primal American when you helped generate me. Thanks for braving all the angry stares, and how Mom's family acted when they found out. Maybe you were used to it from your first marriage, or maybe you couldn't help it, maybe it was some kind of pathology or calling you just had to trust and answer. All I know is now there's me, star seeded and yellow in the freest way possible, like a glow or a solar body, sparring with myself, self-aggrandizing like an emcee, a jazz trio of one. It's not always easy but I'm meant to be. But I'm also so skeptical I sometimes forget... I've been trying to write or find what Sun Ra calls **The Black Myth** or **The Living Myth** or **If you're not a myth whose reality are you.** The more I meditate on it, the more I know it has to do with ideas of the black male, black masculinity, the creative and destructive powers that the trade winds pave into the black male psyche, gender and endlessness. Not a biography derivative of Horus or Osiris, not the falcon who is the bull of his own mother, something more mundane, or with more of a hoodrich gangster lean.

I think Black America needs her own parthenogenerative story of the male who emerged from captivity as a god of rhythm and with the drum has been reprogramming the minds of Americans and deprogramming his own mind, ever since. I'm not sure how to describe the feminine counterpart though; the lived myth of it might be too close to my own/hero/hubris/hybrid/heart. I remember deconstructing the lyrics to I *Loves You, Porgy* and finding myself two-stepping in there, constantly trying to choose between the sane-seeming, safe-seeming man, and the black artist or pimp type of guy (sometimes the artist is the pimp too and sometimes not) but having to choose weather or not to be an agent in someone's healing or inability to heal, the feminine side of the black myth is a lot like me, fatherless, full of the father, **Taurus in the arena of life,** the bull of her own father, maybe she becomes her father's best traits in order to love herself and heal him in the same gesture, legacy work, wish work, prayer, protest, peace—they whistle at her stoic and she remains sure, *Imma keep chanting.* Or maybe she's the vessel of the drum that learns to play itself and makes the men feel superfluous and they lash out and beat on her harder but she can't seem to feel it, which turns them to riveted stone and keel, and they keel. Afraid that she will surpass them, or sure of it. Maybe she's the velvet dark wild energy who you find out also has a domestic side that hums *I've been your slave ever since I've been your babe* over the glowing stove, and it's so confusing people start to study her instead of interact with her, looking for clues into a sanctuary.

So as you can tell I don't have it all figured out yet, I just know we need our own myth as badly as we need our own businesses: record labels, health food stores, publishing houses, and our own ideas, and ideologies and forms and sound and silences. *Shhhhh.*

I think in our case, in the Black American case, any effective mythos will have to be hyper-real, the way color TV looked in the '70s. Maybe it wasn't just the hues and the light spectrums and electro-magnetisms of the machine, but also the colors and textures people were wearing then, the polyesters and polychromes and the chunky polish of pomade on sewn in braids or blown out afros, all the unknown chemicals, all the new imitation food; in the flesh families that felt like cartoons on screen; and all the expensive and cheap laughter as they advertised the new American, Jim Crow, Jim Parrot, broke-down parody, lifestyle to viewers. The Black Myth needs to be that addictive, that slick that corny and that believable. It needs to transcend all media. It needs to surpass television, it needs to feel like some kind of movie that's always being projected into the American climate and improvised on by us until it feels new again, but sharp, surreal, endless, and edgeless, like the alchemy we call Blues Music, and Jazz Music. I think it has a lot to do with our music, the heroes and the gods of the Black Myth are Musicians and Lyricists. Robert Johnson, Louis Armstrong, Sun Ra, Duke Ellington, Ornette Coleman, Rahsaan Roland Kirk, Lester Young, Billie Holiday, Miles Davis, Beyoncé, Kanye, Prince, Michael Jackson, J Dilla, Yasiin Bey, Amiri Baraka, James Baldwin, stay Black. We have to learn how to re-imagine the stories of these giants until they transcend space and time and teach us of the transcendent festival that is Black life in America, but how?

I think it's the mythorealism of my experience of you that makes this so important to me. Or maybe it's my wish to reconcile all of my experiences with black men. To not just cop out and deem my subjective/elective, objective (all three) experiences some sign that some men will always be incorrigible, irresponsible monsters whenever they get ready, that violence is mandatory on the continuum of expressivity, because I don't really believe that. I just think sometimes you guys are still children, having been teased and brutalized for years by the time you encounter a woman you love, you take all of your nightmares and fears out on her or try to make her become them cause that's easier than true identification. I'll have to keep teasing out these ideas until they're not so wrapped up in the evolution of my own ego that they feel like home movies, but I feel like I'm close to beyond my own cover of I Loves You, Porgy . . .

I love you,
Harmony

                                                                    . . U

                                                            100.00
                                                            100.00

                                                            100.00
                                                            100.00

                                                             50.00
                                                             50.00
                                                             50.00
                                                             50.00

                                                            100.00
                                                            100.00

                    CO

            JAY JAMES E   100.00
            SIL MUSIC   50.00
            METRIC MUSIC CO   50.00

            HOLIDAY JAMES E   33.40
        W   CHAMBERS CLIFF   33.30
        W   LEWIS JIMMY   33.30
        P   UNITED ARTISTS MUSIC CO INC   100.00

  8-5   W   HOLIDAY JAMES E   50.00
        W   LEWIS JIMMY   50.00
        P   ASA MUSIC COMPANY   100.00

MY FUNNY VALENTINE IN TIME

Eternity for me has always possessed these immaculate bay windows that look out onto blind alternate takes of the last time I saw my father before he entered that great always on February 15, 1987. A mahogany black man at about 6'3" roused from his habitual afternoon nap for the event: being arrested by a couple of stout white cops at the door of our Iowa home. I had turned him in; I had lied and said it was his brother Percy at our door, my mom's advice, I was five, I was high yellow and what did he do to be so black and blue. But I knew even then how he was a true artist and healer too: a singer, griot, town crier, such wise moans he could make us see our bones and mend them just sitting at his home piano being honest. Famous, fearlessness, anonymous, 52. Maybe the beatings were just him trying to paint my white mother, his second white wife, 25, in his delta of pain and promise or make sure she was his until she would wear it like a tattoo. I believe that to be true. My mother and I both loved him as if it was, we trusted the double scenario of him as a symptom of this country's chronic post-traumatic slave syndrome, and still do. And then sometimes understanding is fatal. That was our special danger there in that house, three half-martyrs to the so-called race problem cheating at our family game of musical chairs and someone had to stand for it: for the interchangeability of tenderness and terror, exhilaration and dread, black and white into silver screen or smoke screen.

  The last words I remember him
saying were *but if you guys leave me I'll die.* My romance doesn't have to have a heart.

I don't think I've ever been numb and I certainly wasn't numb to his plea, I was just certain we would all go on forever being who we are, I wasn't under the bribery in that moment, plus I was five. It was like why it might be easier to write a myth in a language you can only half speak. Or to trust one in that same half-grasped language. All verbs are in the present tense and the conditional if feels absurd and almost violating: *what do you mean* 'if'—promises were like signs of illiteracy and I knew he was too powerful for that finite feeling he enacted then, even as I knew he meant it, he never broke his word, his word never broke him as the internal hymns of powerful men roll off their common speech like prophecy. And the next thing I remember we were on these cots in battered women's shelter, my mom and I. We had a really benevolent social worker and a friend at the shelter with *sleeping sickness* who would fall asleep standing up in the elevator all the time just when we needed to enter the dream like a metronome for our infinite chances and wispy inevitability. We were hiding, I think, from my father's family who lived in the neighborhood and who we knew would be irate about my father's young white second wife having sold him out to the pigs. The race was on.

It wouldn't be long before we would fly to San Diego to be with my grandparents on my mother's side, who I ironically called "the white grandma and the white grandpa" cause of their pitch white hair, not cause I understood that the race was on. My mom about eight months pregnant at the time. It wouldn't be long after that, that I would watch my mom slide down their hallway wall weeping like one of those dimly lit daytime TV ads for anti-depressants, at the news of my father's eternity and all I could say at that casually intense, impatient age was *It'll be okay.* Stay, Valentine, stay. Three days later my sister Sara was born.

SONG TITLE	ASSOCIATED PARTIES
IF I CAN'T CHANGE THE WORLD (DO	PUB: JOBETE MUSIC CO INC
	PUB: OLD BROMPTON ROAD MUSIC
STAY WITH ME	WRI: HOLIDAY, JIMMY
	PUB: JOBETE MUSIC CO INC
IT'S GOOD TO BE HOME	WRI: OLD BROMPTON ROAD MUSIC
STOP	WRI: HOLIDAY, JIMMY
	PUB: JOBETE MUSIC CO INC
ELIZABETH	WRI: OLD BROMPTON ROAD MUSIC
THE BIG TOWN	WRI: HOLIDAY, JIMMY
	HOLIDAY, ELIZABETH
	PUB: JOBETE MUSIC CO INC
HAPPINESS	WRI: OLD BROMPTON ROAD MUSIC
THE BOOK OF MY LIFE	WRI: HOLIDAY, JIMMY
	WOODS, MARCIA
	PUB: JOBETE MUSIC CO INC
HOW DID THE RAIN GET IN	WRI: OLD BROMPTON ROAD MUSIC
THE TWO OF US	WRI: HOLIDAY, JIMMY
KEEP ON TALKIN'	WRI: KILGORE, THEOLA
	PUB: JOBETE MUSIC CO INC
I BEEN LOVEJACKED	PUB: OLD BROMPTON ROAD MUSIC
THE WORLD WE LIVE IN	WRI: HOLIDAY, JIMMY
LET NO ONE CATCH YOU CRYING	PUB: JOBETE MUSIC CO INC
	PUB: OLD BROMPTON ROAD MUSIC
THERE'LL BE NO MORE CRYING	WRI: HOLIDAY, JIMMY
LISTEN TO MY STORY	PUB: JOBETE MUSIC CO INC
	PUB: OLD BROMPTON ROAD MUSIC
	PUB: ABC MUSIC CO INC
WEEP FOR THEM (WEEP FOR ME)	WRI: HOLIDAY, JIMMY
LIVE TO RUN AGAIN	WRI: KING, LEE ANN
	PUB: JOBETE MUSIC CO INC
	PUB: OLD BROMPTON ROAD MUSIC
	ABC MUSIC
WHEN I'M LOVING YOU	WRI: HOLIDAY, JIMMY
	RARIE, JONNE
	PUB: SWITZLER, PAUL
	PUB: JOBETE MUSIC CO INC
	OLD BROMPTON ROAD MUSIC
I NEVER FELT THIS WAY BEFORE	WRI: ABC MUSIC
LOVE IS A GIFT	WRI: HOLIDAY, JIMMY
WORRIED	PUB: JOBETE MUSIC CO INC
LOVE WON'T LIVE HERE (SINCE YO	WRI: OLD BROMPTON ROAD MUSIC
	ABC MUSIC
YOU'RE GETTING BETTER	WRI: HOLIDAY, JIMMY
	ROGERS, ELEEN
I'M GONNA LOVE YOU	PUB: JOBETE MUSIC CO INC

The Holiday Family

Here we are. It was great,
seeing everybody and we'll
be back soon. Next time
maybe Harmony Lynn will be
walkin and talkin!
Take care Love

Susan and Larry Holiday
MOM) DAD)

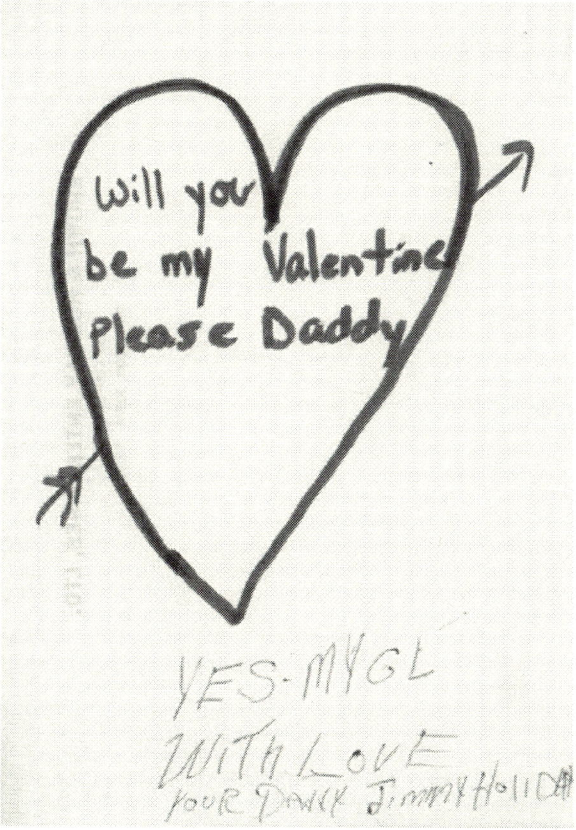
Will you
be my Valentine
Please Daddy
YES-MY GL
WITH LOVE

Let's try again. The last time I saw my father he was running through a field of mute purple flowers holding on to that pale brown Stetson hat he always wore with one hand and flipping the invisible the bird with the other. Everyone coughs up blood in the back of the ambulance on the way to the hospital, it's tradition. Flashback to the precise moment I first waved to him from the white horse on the carnival carousel one time, cotton candy ink on my gloriously tiny fingers as I turned the corner crooking my neck to watch my favorite audience, magic. We're moving forward toward our myth. I'll pick the cotton candy if you sing to me a blues about it. Dye hue number 7 blue. But don't use that word. Rhyme with idle. Don't worship idols. Don't talk about color anymore, either. Eternity for men.

DEAR DAD,

The white horse anchored and rose with such likelihood each go-around on the carousel and I felt like a queen up there alone between whites and lights, a little amber music. How I kept looking for your Stetson towering above all those mediocre heads and herds at the carnival. Are we cannibals, are we a clan of heroes, or villains, or both? It's indecipherable. Excellence is a threat here but we go ahead with it. Both sides now. Sometimes I wonder how you and my grandfather, mom's dad, would have really gotten on together under the right chances. I mean, he had his qualms with your marriage to mom, her being so much younger, you being a black genius, he's a genius too, all the obvious clashes. But let's say you were both side by side on the frontlines of one of those atrocious wars this country recruited each of you for, let's imagine a black man and a white man born five or six years apart, side by side in fatigues. Pretend we all already know that black man is fixin' to marry the white man's daughter back home, so they're family, technically, united in the bloodlines of the coming years. Would they chat about growing up, sublime, transcendent clichés that whisper *save us*, their respective mothers' home cooking, the women they'd loved and unloved, the bustle of hometown stillness, the trust they'd built for one another, what it felt like for two writers to point guns at innocent strangers, or burn currency, or see spirits chumming around in he mud and weep beer and snuff, what it means to sing your way to freedom, the tolls, the little sunflowers that make it all worth how. Seems likely they would fall in love, agape love, right on the scene, embrace and make monotone tears from a their two trembling smiles. Imagining is remembering, imagining is remembering.

We all love one another madly, your daughter,
Harmony

DEAR DAD,

To keep my mind agile and to keep it from fixating on the souls of black folk, I study the most antique systems of thought I can find, looking for a new grammar of the human soul, knowing this paradigm of black and white is childish or adolescent, the ego's way of hiding from more universal truths about the self. I'm on that black hippie shit I guess. The image of Mom stopping at the juice bar for wheatgrass shots on the way to my ballet classes when I was kid is etched in my mind, and her love of Enya during that era. Wine, wheatgrass, and Enya. This, ironically, just gives me extra fodder for the black myth I'm always working to write or perform or deliver or habit or be. Last summer I got into reading about the glands and the chakras and what organs they correspond to and what that correspondence means for us, for our well being as people. I learned how the current position of the planet is such that the serpent energy, the potential for the flow of light up the vertebrae of earth and so of every being on its beautiful surface, is rising, and now that yoga is all the rave in west, we talk about it like experts and charlatans, and we shed numb words for it in casual conversations. It's a sexual energy that can be transmuted into a creative one if not abused or misused, if kept pure, if controlled. And if not controlled, the whole nervous system is in jeopardy because the energy is there either way we treat it. As a result lots of people are having nervous breakdowns and lots of nation-states are erupting into revolutionary struggle. More miracles seem to show up in the everyday and it seems like the border between a miracle and a disaster is thinning and like that's a good thing, forcing people to be braver, to take risks and speak out in honor of what they truly believe in. Love is Everywhere as Pharoah Sanders puts it. Love is in us all.

But what's really on my mind today is what that all means for modern love. I've always wondered what my romances would be like if I didn't fancy the myth so well, but now that the myth seems to be within reach I think the real needs to be guarded with equal enthusiasm. Either way I've got a great talent for falling in love, the all or nothing kind, it's either love or indifference for me, with most matters. I practice it on men who are too much like you to be like you, and I practice with discipline and art and in the mirror over the Six Secret Syllables and the Seven Windows. The Tao, you know, Wu-Tang's savior and maybe one of mine also, where I fall in love with how it all began, trust my center, all that indispensible shit you just want to throw against the wall some days, and those are the days it's most valuable.

And I'm finally reading the Bible, the Oxford Annotated version to keep a critical distance from monotheism. I'm not surprised that what Christians call the devil, the evildoer, is a guy who started out as lead angel, angel of Music no less. Maybe it's a fear of pleasure, or an envy of the joys of the artist, especially the musician. Or maybe people got tired of being seduced and started blaming music for their very desires, turned virtue into vice, appreciation into delirium, with a turn of phrase. I listen to too much Jazz music to trust that kind of holding back or backlash. I'm smack in the middle of each and every moment looking for its most lyrical veer. All this kinesis called Jazz sees, are alternatives, it's a loyal kind of promiscuous you don't encounter often outside of the music's courageous tones. But there's this theory that Lucifer was a child of Venus, the angel of music, and that Satan who was the projection of Saturn, was Lucifer's shadow. Maybe so, right? Why not. Lucifer is deemed the morning star, the first good of each new day. Lucifer, sun of the morning. I've been reading theories like these and decoding myths by accident, more toward getting back to ours.

It feels like together we too are children of Venus, we wield it with tremendous grace and disdain for the slumped over types whose hearts fade into patient delusion on purpose, wasting the transformative power on stasis. I'm not sure if I'm a believer but I'm starting to look closer and see the dopamine in purple and the dope in blue and the Bible in Hebrew and the mystic brew. I read Joseph Campbell and study Eastern religions and trace my skin back to Upper Egypt the Dogon Tribe and Sicilian Mafia creed, and tease the numb out with the pride of these untold open secrets. It's a beautiful and alien feeling. I'm deepening, I'm tired of mediocre Uncle Tom-type men pretending to be artists when all the create are more slogans for the least challenging most boring and unexamined American life. There are plenty of men like that who think their identity is a "success" for it too, think I should be impressed by their acts. I'm rejecting them. I'm depending on me again.

Your joyous daughter,
Harmony

                                                                    50.00
                                                                    50.00
                                                                   100.00

                                                                    50.00
                                                                    50.00
                                                                    50.00
                                                                    50.00

                    JACKIE   50.00
                 JAMES E   50.00
              MUSIC CORP   100.00

          HOLIDAY JAMES E   100.00
          METRIC MUSIC COMPANY   100.00

   16-4   W   HOLIDAY JAMES E   100.00
              P   METRIC MUSIC CO   100.00

 026488-3   W   HOLIDAY JAMES E   100.00
              P   UNITED ARTISTS MUSIC CO INC   100.00

 019143-9   W   DE SHANNON JACKIE   33.20
              W   HOLIDAY JAMES E   33.20

One more time.

The last time I saw my father he was tore up on and off his lithium like a radio signal sitting at the piano bench half asleep writing a song about me he called *Midnight Girl*, this gigantic elegy for himself that I could come to mean, transcending. Happy elegy. Carefree elegy. The meek ain't gonna inherit shit, 'cause I'll take it, elegiac leadership. *You can't be with me, 'cause you're a midnight girl, that no one can ever own, 'cause you belong to the world…*

DEAR DAD,

I had a dream about you last night. A chant running through it: *Today is the day that you give your heart to Jesus, today is the day that you give your life to Allah, today is the day that give your heart to Ra, today is the day that you give your mind Osiris, today is the day that you give your heart to Shiva, today is the day that you give your heart to Jesus, today is the day that you give your heart to Jah*—the preacher kept going...

With such sweet devotion. And though you couldn't read you taught me to read in this version, the phonetics, the fanatics who didn't make good friends—you muted to the preaching and went into a lecture on the loom of language and made me promise to master its culled spin its aspen air its clamor of hint merriment as you burrowed your knees into run

No, that's not all of it. The last time I saw my father, gun in one hand, cross in the other, don't panic. These are the two objects beneath all modern love buzzing like a partially-flipped light switch, coming to terms and then leaving terms for speechlessness or to function. They switch hands, the heart opens and flutters and you tell your first born under a lucky sign how one thing leads to another...

SEE-THROUGH RIVERS

Erykah Badu has a song brilliantly/cryptically/comically, titled, *Fall in Love/Your Funeral* on her *New Amerykah Part Two* LP, and the song begins: **you better go back the way you came, wrong way, if you stay, prepare to have your shit rearranged, the way I say.** Just as ceremoniously the hook chants, *you don't wanna fall in love with me, uhuh, no way.* We can seize the opportunity to hear this as a most generous warning dispatched from Black America to White America; and to the world at large. When White America fell in Love with Blackness and tried to hold it captive as a means of accessing and appropriating its fruits, so-called Whiteness was re-arranged just as Africanness was. When my mother fell in Love with my father not only were both of them altered, I came forth as an emblem of that mutually re-arranging capacity, let's say, as all children of mixed and re-mixed race do and will. Barack Obama. We gaze back at the distracted Mississippi River polluted with capital, and I'm scrolling my father's mind in search of something cleansing or recognizable or a song to cry or rove in like a pliant animal—not a mule in sight for miles—

DEAR DAD,

Now for the topic I've been avoiding. Some things just aren't abstract or distant enough. I had this ridiculous emotional affair with a married man for about a year. It felt like longer. Maybe because he was a writer too so there were so many words and tones it felt like touring the ages. I think I did it as a means of getting over my true love for that other guy, but it mostly taught me that that guy is family, to love him more, catapulted me right back into his happy arms. This married dude, he's eleven years older than me and married to a dusty woman whose spirit seems to be hiding from her and slurring her wandering eyes. Could be that he snatched it out of her over all those years. I can't be sure if he's a sociopath or just a broken man but maybe both, or maybe he's just another bored phony nigga hoping to vampire in on this wondrous blood of ours. No chance. When are they going to understand you gotta have it to get it. I think his dusty wife was in on the attempt too. The whole time it felt like a couple of mediocre parasites who knew they had struck gold but whose eyes were too dull to see gold, bodies too toxic to assimilate the mineral. We would share words and music mostly. So much, so many. I think it made me feel safe that he was unavailable, don't think I ever really wanted him, just had something to learn from him as archetype. And every time I gave him a piece of music it felt dirty, like passing lucent material direct to the stain of Saturn's murky shadow or ectoplasm, but he was tall and seemed intelligent, so I overlooked it. I lashed out at him for his sociopathic-seeming complacency every few months until it finally became so lame that the cycle couldn't sustain any more panthers or lashes from either side.

Phew. But there was something traumatic about it. The fact that some part me of me cared about him. Then he tried to sabotage me like a true saturnine kind, out of guilt or malice or just ignorance, his gleaming weakness , neurosis he disguises as casualness. He broke a universal law out of some infantile jealousy or yearning for revenge against his own mother who he thinks he was the bull of, who he speaks about like a two-syllable stranger. Now I think he thinks I'm his mother. And he's mad that he just made me stronger, more beautiful, and more impossible for him to have. I'd blame your divinity for saving me and then forcing me divine that way, forcing me to write you and to become even better at being me, but I'd mean thank you. Herbie Hancock's I *Thought It Was You* comes into my mind like a beautiful foul ball no one catches but the camera. It's on tape. Another black body on videotape. There's more I could say, but later. Just stay vigilant with me. And thank you for taking all those risks in life, proving the true value and valor of your heart, not biting on white America's expectations of black artists, but exceeding them, and making it to the top too, and ever higher. So that I know one thing from another. I'm too proud of you to stay under the spell of a phony, though for a while it felt like a thing to do. I'm not going to pretend you always treated women right, but thank you for not being him.

Love,
Harmony

Love is war(m)(n)ed for Miles

There's more. I think there's more. The last time I saw my father he was driving me everywhere like a purpose. He wore that same pale Stetson and said *You okay...* it wasn't a question. The car disappeared and I woke up in a tree with a craving for drums, spunky tambourines, new associations, the burning candle, to be as delicate as I am and so tough I disperse when you try and touch me with envy and I turn into him for then, he offers up all of his weapons, the guns, the getaway cars, and I chose the voice again. If you conflate intelligence with repression, and reward decorum like a triumph you'll understand the Western view of tragedy as the highest form of art and aspire toward it and that would be tragic. Wear the red dress with the black spirit and the white privilege, fuck everybody who asks you what you're mixed with or just lovingly ask yourself, what are you mixed with?

TRDBCAT   11/19/04   TITLE REGISTRATION CATALOGUE

NAME: HOLIDAY JAMES E   NCODE: 5111810 SC
REQUESTED NAME: HOLIDAY JAMES E   TYPE: COMPOSER/AUT

        S O N G   T I T L E   ASSOCIATED PARTIES

                                      PUB:JOBETE MUSIC CO INC
                                         OLD BROMPTON ROAD MU
        STAY WITH ME   WRI:HOLIDAY, JIMMY **35**
                                      PUB:JOBETE MUSIC CO INC
                                         OLD BROMPTON ROAD M

DEAR DAD,

There was this burning, he got this burning. He married her. She stole from him, ransacked his spirit looking for melanin. She sold his house, his cars, she cannibalized the daughters of women he had affairs with (polygamy is only fair), she bought cocaine and brandy and a man with the proceeds. He beat her like a pillow, no, that's not enough, he pounded her as though pulp looking for, seeking its—fiction. Substance and light landed in one place most nights like the miracle's supra minions, and white supremacy being what it in this country, she got by with (it), and melanin being what it is, worldwide, him being an exceptionally melinated man especially compared to her chandelier, spray tan ivory, he got by, he got buyed, he got bide. Jack Johnson, Jack Johnson. Jack Johnson. The boxer sent to prison for getting rich and marrying a white woman. Some say melanin is chaos. Then some say, *Well then, nigga, this goes out to chaos.* Language gives me an angelic echo the mind can then locate and float on. That's the story of your first marriage as told by the talking book. I shook it and white powder fell out and I held my breath and screamed backwards looking for these words.

I love you,
Harmony

HE'S A RUNNER

Suppose fugitivity is genetic, or so interlocked with the black spirit in this land by now that running is the new normal and so a form of stasis. I've still got that baton in mind, that relay, that classically hip and gallant dash. That cavalier shit we've mastered. We start off talking about looking and grow into a discussion of being found, suppose, superimposed or hologrammed in the phantom run/position.

Once upon a time I felt ghosts were romantic. The clipping off of phrases you can't complete in a tantrum or drum from a one-planet spectrum. It can be as though the ghost is a history of the future and if it's your father and you read Freud with impossibly suspicious eyes huddled around the goodbye like total angels, kettles, all-knowing valves, you can't help but be a narcissist and an addict, addicted to replicas of your father who, in exemplifying him, make you more beautiful to yourself, in both memory and imagination. For me to go find my father has meant to fall in love or infatuation with black artists who are a lot like him. This search morphs from being about one man, to being about at least three, from being about my vigilance to being about where it meets with blindness, from being about Saturn to being about Venus, from being about love to being about where love equals desire: a rare alcove of beauty, truth, and the riveting unknown. It's always about love, obsession, indifference, admitting their relationship to one another. Warm like a relief, warm like a warning, warm like winning your heart back from an imposter and getting to tell him *Nigga, you ain't mysterious,* just as you admit it to yourself, in a frenzied, I'm gonna leave yo jive ass, jot on a napkin. Next of kin, next of kin.

DEAR DAD,

I have this short film in mind, or maybe it's a story called, It *Wasn't Me*; or It *Wasn't Me Either*. It's about a white girl who runs away from home and decides to become a prostitute. But she decides to become a black prostitute. She dresses as a black woman night and day/day and night, and all of her clients are so happy and fooled and she learns what it feels like to be called beautiful and not believe it, or be called *pretty nigger girl* as he unbuckles his belt. What fantasies they share! Her only ambivalence is when she falls for it herself, down on her knees and she can't remember the hidden edge of her own skin and where it all begins is in the memory, which is of the future too. She's out to cure something; some bolted window in her spirit is puckering toward spring with the lazy poise of spinning vinyl on one of the futuristic machines that reminds her of a rhinoceros. She gets closer and closer. She holds the speaker to her heart like a pledge every time. And then one night her father, her ivory white father, pulls up to her in his Benz, and he doesn't recognize her as he says, *baby, c'mon in and show me...* he stutters a little candid arousal, *get in and show me what you got.*

Ebony and Ivory,
Harmony

I FALL IN LOVE TOO EASILY

No, I think it went more like when blame is obsolete and the breeze is so light it aches like a cure who do you love? What do you love about them? Forget everything else. Become that.

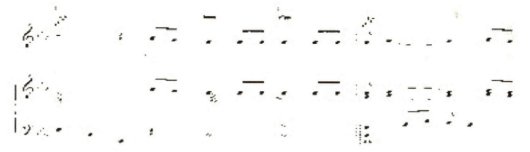

VELVET ROPE ROBOTS

It starts very sensually, essentialism and good gin. If you fall in love with a famous musician named Otis and it's all very old school like tuning into your own personal frequency on the radio, and your father was a famous musician so it feels like some griot legacy meant-to-be shit and your hope for the conversation on earth is fatuous and invincible, libido and soul. It doesn't matter that he's in the studio for fourteen hours a day, that dinner plans are made and cancelled and made again and cancelled again. Your eyes are watching god, but they're closed. You're in love, not with the unavailability but with the genius, the tender and palpable wizardry, the fact the he's the easiest person in the world to be around and he feels the same way about you, the fact that you feel no grasping or jealousy about living across the country from one another, you in New York and he in L.A. You're from L.A., you grew up there, your friends and family are elated when you start visiting more often. You take them to parties and concerts and meet him at those and it's ridiculous and perfect but something's off, something ain't totally right. He says you should meet his parents. You're a writer, a poet, with a book to finish and a career to begin and to figure out what's off do the obvious/most cliché natural black invention and flee to Paris for a couple months where all you do is miss him and think about the relationship between your past and your future as part of the myth, time begins to feel like one long sublime tragi-comedic moment of truth. Maybe the thing that's off is a factor of what's recurred, how after years of avoiding falling in love with men exactly like your father, you venture in that direction and feel the pressure of your child self knocking on the window of your soul with a mixture of delight and warning. Whatever, you're in love. He's in love. It's simple. You know he has children and don't even mind, he's vowed he's not involved with the mothers (yep plural) of them time and again. You don't judge. We have no guilt and we are ungovernable. You pay it no mind, feeling like you could even love his children you love him so much. Only when one of his friends warns you that he's engaged on the down low, to the mother of his second child, do you see the world in audio-color. Ahhhh, *there's the world!*, back on its axis, you tilt a little and then straighten up and fly right, shit fly left if you have to, just fly. And you love him anyways, still, like a soulmate, in agreement, in a minted circumstance that changes your understanding of desire, of love, of commitment, of Freud, of understanding itself, of the angle the black myth can sustain when it's active, when it's a living myth. But your searchlight begins to dimly flicker again. Pieces of song emerge and immerse as light source.

Put Some Weave in Your Hair, Y'all Suckas - Lil B

Never give Give a sucka Sucker an Even Break an even break - Archie Shepp

You Ain't Seen Me Right? - Killer of Sheep

Morning Bird - Sade

If you set me free, I will not run / I will not run   Fugitivity is imminent in the thing but manifest transversally - Fred Moten

DEAR DAD,

Are you and Debby at peace? I hope so. Wonder if she knows how to believe that had you known the woman you had an affair with was pregnant you would have gladly been with her from day one, instead of learning of her birth three years in, after she was put up for adoption and subject to abusive foster parents, and rescuing her then. You took responsibility for all of your children, you did it with pride. I wasn't there to see the other side of it back then, but imagining is remembering.

On the topic of affairs, there must be a part of me that sees that as part of the paradigm I'm in or something. Like a one-wife life story feels like no story at all, feels like pandering or something. Though I see the beauty there, my grandparents, mom's parents, attain that beauty in their marriage but what they have feels obsolete, genuine beyond the tone of most humans walking around today. And as mom so astutely put it, people had time apart back then, men went away to fight in wars, romance was built into the suspense of that, increased intensity, and without all these machines we have now, telepathy and intuition really amounted to something much more substantial than what we know of them today. Who knows. Maybe in my subconscious fairy tale I'm a second wife, the one a man gets it right with, the mature post-denial love story about soul and not etiquette. The vessel, the silver lining, the golden time. Maybe that's still with me, why me and you are at peace, because I come from that energy. Whatever it is, I'm alive with it and that feels like an accomplishment for all paradigms, beyond right and wrong. A lucky threat like that Spike Lee line from *Do The Right Thing*: "You're lucky the Black man has a loving heart." That's how I feel sometimes, that's the tie the binds us to and of our music no matter what, I feel. The question nods into will.

More love,
Harmony

			RALPH
			LIDAY JAMES E
			ROBERTS BOB
			SUNNY SKIES MUSIC CO
		W	HOLIDAY JAMES E
		W	LEWIS JIMMY
		W	CHAMBERS CLIFF
		P	METRIC MUSIC CO
	49-024726-6	W	HOLIDAY JAMES E
		P	CHARLES RAY ENTER INC
		P	VERSIL MUSIC
ER	49-030474-8	W	DE SHANNON JACKIE
		W	HOLIDAY JAMES E
		W	MYERS RANDY JAMES
		P	UNART MUSIC CORP
YOUR LOVE	49-026050-9	W	HOLIDAY JAMES E
		P	ASA MUSIC COMPANY
OW	49-028437-8	W	HOLIDAY JAMES E
		W	CHAMBERS CLIFF
		P	UNART MUS CORP
ON T BOTHER ME	50-017993-5	W	HOLIDAY JAMES E
		P	VERSIL MUSIC
AKES IT	50-016278-3	W	HOLIDAY JAMES E
		W	EGNOIAN
		W	FLOYD
		P	DRIVE IN MUSIC CO INC
		P	BONNYVIEW MUSIC CORP
A LIE	50-018781-9	W	HOLIDAY JAMES E
		W	CHARLES RAY
		P	TANGERINE MUS CORP
LITTLE KINDNESS	50-020987-6	W	DE SHANNON JACKIE
		W	HOLIDAY JAMES E

DEAR DAD,

We were fighting to get the publishing rights to your songs back. Debby and I learned all there is to know about Work-for-Hire contract law and instead of getting angry, though we were angry and offended and entangled and the bend in the river went blind for a while as we learned and re-mastered the new form of slavery, how it's written into law and everything, but we remained calm and kept fighting. We won that way. Today is the day that your songs came back to us. We won, we one today. That's how we won.

Makes me proud,
Harmony

DEAR DAD,

Some days all I think about is love and money. How one becomes the other so easily. All I think about is God and Me, rich spirited and in love, juicing vegetables and making music and pushing luck to the limit where it becomes a destiny, a sin, a song, a win, a relief, the tender clang of cymbals around the blow. All I think about is me some days. I'm selfish, fuck it. All I think about is you because you are me, because all of this thinking carries the vibration of love and radiance, treasons that save our souls for sin. I mix Himalayan pink salt and blue green algae and throw it over avocado and Miles' *Blue in Green* and *thinking about the dreams as they are happening*. Rappin Black, Rappin Black. Kin things. How the blood is what it does.

The blood of the thing

          is the truth

of the thing/   *we came to be addicted to blood;*

                    we came to be addicted to truth

For love or money,
Harmony

DEAR DAD,

Thanks. Look out far Sara too, and for Mom, and me and Debby too. We all need you more than we know.

Love,
Harmony

DEAR DAD,

Debby told me about the time a guy was harassing her in L.A. How you arranged to have her pretend to meet him at a hotel and when he got there you were waiting and pulled some Kung Fu moves on him to the extent that he hobbled out speechless and who knows if anyone ever heard from him again. This remembrance is an invocation. Thanks for protecting us. I think about how much that means. One time in the middle of telling me a lie I didn't know was a lie, my true love guy fell down and rolled down a mound of tar in the parking lot where we were waiting for our car, and I felt you there, guarding, ardent, swinging, no pardon, knowing pardon, knowing when. I think about how the word *crazy* is often tinged with envy, in English at least, there's not built-in wink acknowledged, and the behavior that gets tossed into the word is often heroic simile for savior or riddle for healer, or lore for lord. Then I consider how if I call you a hero/my savior and the show must go on, everything shifts toward love and redemption. The ugly words seize and crumble. Happiness is easy. Our mosaics bleed backwards and make a sun and heirs, raid our hunts with the everything glares of mercy—I see you there, water gathers on my gaze and scatters. Your heart isn't haunted anymore. My heart isn't haunted anymore.

Lucky us,
Harmony

DEAR DAD,

I've been investigating theories about how the elaborate way the Hebrew alphabet folds into flames must mean the language itself vibrates faster and could tell us a lot about our own hearts. Yours and mine, one healing the other. It's not that we're in a rush or a hurry or any fixation on urgency beyond truth, it's more that we trust ourselves more often than the average soul, and the more that trust happens the more fire we grasp and transmute into song. I never knew writing to you like this would feel so true like a kind of divine emptiness. With all this fire though, I've started turning toward the Tao again, learning how is distribute the energy among my glands and organs so it doesn't play out like false adrenaline. They play the organs like instruments, an acoustics of anatomy... *Shhhhh*, they say to the green hued liver, and its flame steadies into BenBen tree.

Since when is it okay for a black person to ponder trees without thoughts of medicine or simian. I think its finally okay and I love the way that oak feels in the ground of my imagination. I love our Strange Humors. I love that Amiri Baraka line from his poem *Dope* where he snatches the onus back so quietly it's remote and confrontational at the same oath, promising, *And what we do we will do.*

Black Art,
Harmony

THE RHETORIC OF URGENCY / NIGGA THIS GOES OUT TO CHAOS

I wanna be reeeeee-eeeea deee *I wanna be ready* *I wanna be reeeeeeeedee* *ready* *to put on* *my long* *white robe* , the spiritual begins, and the dancers in the famous Alvin Ailey choreography, sharp amber spotlight on their almond skin in white cotton, undulate skyward on the *I wanna* and collapse as earth angels on the *be ready* in pre-break-dance era articulate/isolation as if to suggest readiness is twofold and too fluent in itself to utter its laws in common/grammar, a matter of rising up and digging in at the same time/ timber/timbre. Sin and repent/sin and repent, in a kind of cosmically charged circuit that adds up to perfect timing and perfect pitch. It's very *I'm not asking you I'm telling you*. Humble arrogance, or confident humbleness. It's how we keep ourselves immortal and fragile (intuitive) at the same jolt. It's how we blind (bling) the myth by becoming it.

DEAR DAD,

How about the time your brought your demo all the way from New Orleans to Chicago, to Ray Charles' office and headquarters in Los Angeles, and then when his secretary said he had no time to meet you or to listen, how you sat there every day from 8 to 8 for an entire week until on Friday he said to his secretary *Let the nigga in,* and you guys became fast and lasting friends and collaborators. It's hard to really forgive him for trying to not pay us royalties for the songs of his you wrote, for trying to buy your catalog back from us for a hundred dollars like we were oblivious, but hey, we worked it out, so now I can muse on the tenderness between you and him. Is that true about the time you wrote the song *Hey, Mister* together, protesting Nixon's overall shade and dominion, and his administration asked radio stations to take it off the air? The heir prepares for takeoff on such a truth, I fly to it. It sounds true to me, or resonates that way, based on the surveillance state we live in today in this country. Is it true that you met Nixon himself and rested your cowboy boots on his desk in the Oval Office? I believe that too, another hue for the book of laughter and forgetting. The truth feels soft in my heart today, and limitless. Thanks for that.

Love and bravery,
Harmony

DEAR DAD,

It all began very innocently. Love of the forbidden being embedded in the DNA of every man in this territory, which, as all of your recording contracts read "shall be the universe." Such a gorgeous/hideous phrase *the territory shall be the universe*. So you fell in love with my mother, probably not just because she was ivory or olive, or all about it, but that may have helped the arousal, the rule that all we break to mend. And then, what happened? It's all a mystery, all mistreated in the mythocracy. I remember that time she walked into the grocery store to buy me some red Lifesavers, all I would eat because of trauma or stubborn ways. Today I fast for health a couple times a year, maybe then too innately. The well of brute in my bluest throat chakra, and nudges us from Sanskrit to the unscripted slang of true hearts. Anyhow, and as you and I sat in our van outside of the store you asked, *Should we leave her?* There it is! I found it! Such discoveries words breed. The multicolored trace of my loves as they originate in the subconscious. Now I crave and elicit that question from new men, and every time the same answer.

With all of her trauma, by the time she was 28, mom was a pretty solid warrior. Cocaine and wheatgrass and wine and teaching English to NBA players' sons, and flirting with their fathers and single and beautiful and into health food and meditation and cocaine and wine. Can't you feel it rotate in the spine like a saving grace. Pretty much a regular supernatural human waking up to the known unknown. Melanin is chaos, the best kind of clay, and there we were, her melinated daughters, boss and ripe fruit, righteous and wicked too, a beautiful family. And somehow, she knew just what to do, even when we didn't take her seriously and found her more friend or even enemy than parent, she was secretly training us to be perfect. Our Kenyan baby sisters, our Ailey of the West Coast Dance Center where we spent hours and hours every week, learning how to be black with a white mother, learning how to white with a black father, learning the rocket love of the double mask unmasked. Only in Los Angeles could we have learned it with so much sun in our mouths. So much ennui. Pronounced *on we*. We were on!

And today, me now around the age she was back then. Hen, hen, hen, hen, red hen. Today I finally understand the levels and layers and lures of her genius. I finally note the tone in a man's voice when he talks about his mother, as a hint about his mental health. I finally get how important it is to understand one's mother. I finally understand her. And love her as friend, as a kind of hero, as a pure, vain, ridiculous but so intelligent it pierces through even her self-abnegation, heart. Granted, we still have our differences, the record is not over yet, the record is endless, but I can finally listen to it, all the way from track one to the end of side one and onto these new sides, with delighted, comprehensive ears. You made a good choice, you chose a good woman, just as wild and dangerous as you, and just as healing, like a truce in the immeasurable equation may the first spark of love between you and her live on the record that I forever am. There's that. An American family, a new reach in the word mafia. The *Ahhhhhaaa* in there. How it stretches out. I can finally sigh with poise, a whole lot of love and the realization that there's something beyond forgiveness, where you go into the psyche and unblame it, liberate it from associations without letting them run a muck either, reassemble your awareness of the spaces between atoms, become elegant for it, vast distances expand and contract on the one, and there's no more pain to forgive. What is all this joy and justice.

What love is,
Harmony

DEAR DAD,

I read that if you can hold a thought in your head for 17 entire seconds, just that one thought, that it becomes a reality/duality/free/true, finds form through sustained vibration. That's all the black magic I need today. In the IChing, the ancient Book of Changes comprised of 64 hexagrams each containing 6 permutations, the 17th hexagram is for following, falling in love, so it makes a lot of sense. The number 17, the frequency of it, must create the conditions for follow-through, for coming through, adding up to the infinite figure 8. So here goes.

In other news, some days very few things feel worthy of a complete 17 seconds of thought energy. And other days the whole thought process needs redistribution into 17-second increments. Today the construction outside my window was so atrocious even blasting Miles' Tokyo concert didn't quell the disturbance. I finally went to shut the window but it came out of its frame and tumbled into me like a dream, pane and glass but no sound or blood. Ice on my forehead as I thought about the symbolism. Today's letter to you is an improvisation with drill and bulldozer accompaniment, me on bells and wordless vocals. Trying to banish trifling Negros from my 17-second increments like a true high yellow swan reinstating her mojo or window. It's an ensemble, a quintet, a tête-à-tête with self. It rebuilds me the way gazing at the letters of ancient alphabets does, forces my mind to believe again. Forces the will and subconscious to reunion. I guess I'll have to keep doing this. I want to. Need, too. I don't believe in the western model of therapy but I've been through enough with black men and black myths that I need to believe there are some practices that can lure them and me too, out of posttraumatic slave syndrome and into something a little healthier. Sometimes I think it's a matter of tracing polygamy back to it roots in West Africa, where a man has as many wives as he can afford and takes care of them all, and where a queen has her court. In the U.S. it's all the polygamy with none of the responsibility on either side. I'm not claiming innocence, I've been as attracted to the Porgy archetype as I have to the pimp, depends on my level of hubris at the time I meet them, and on theirs. Maybe one of the protagonists of the black myth is a reformed pimp with a wife in every major U.S. city. That would at least be semi-accurate. Hmmmph. That would at least remind us how laughing and crying are opposites of the same energy. I'm not sure how to wrap this series up neatly besides by promising to keep writing, and to keep writing to you. Maybe not every day, maybe once a week is enough. This way maybe next time I'm tempted to love a no-good man, or trust a faulty mythos, the antibodies, the immunity will have built up in me like a drum pattern around these reflections or confessions and I'll remember how I'm as free as I wanna be. And this way maybe I'll just be the Black Myth, telling my story fast.

Love,
Harmony

```
I KNOW YOU KNOW IT              WRI:HOLIDAY, JIMMY
                                   GUILLORY STEVE
                                PUB:JOBETE MUSIC CO INC
                                   OLD BROMPTON ROAD MUSIC
I NEED A HAND-UP (DON'T WANT A  WRI:HOLIDAY, JIMMY
                                PUB:JOBETE MUSIC CO INC
                                   OLD BROMPTON ROAD MUSIC
                                   ABC MUSIC
I NEVER FELT THIS WAY BEFORE    WRI:HOLIDAY, JIMMY
                                PUB:JOBETE MUSIC CO INC
                                   OLD BROMPTON ROAD MUSIC
                                   ABC MUSIC
I WON'T DO WITHOUT YOUR LOVE    WRI:HOLIDAY, JIMMY
                                PUB:JOBETE MUSIC CO INC
                                   OLD BROMPTON ROAD MUSIC
                                   ABC MUSIC
```

DEAR DAD,

I had a dream about you last night. You sang to me the kind emblems (sang, root for sanguine for blood/kin, but also angel, but also…)

There comes a time to wake up to what's happening,
there comes a time to get out of what's happening,
I love you more than what's happening.

All of a sudden there was this huge audience flocking into my dream to hear you sing to me and then you handed me the song, and joined the audience and I had to sing it and I woke up jazz singing it and I keep adding new verses every show and everything is whole and groovy, lotus, lotus, lotus, the voice so low it aches of joy and justice. What is all this joy and justice?

Happier than the midnight sun, your daughter,
Harmony

ASKING THE RIGHT QUESTIONS

When's the last time you spoke to your father? What did you say? What did he say? Is there anything you've never been able to say, cause no one ever asked you the right question? Do you believe in God? What does God look like? What does your father look like? Why do you love him? Who is your mother? What were her dreams as a child? Has she been living them? What is a tribe? What is a drum? How do you mend a broken heart, using a tribe and a drum and a broken camera? What is the difference between a prayer and a spell? What is an artist? What is a black artist? What is the role of black artists during late capitalism? Who does it serve? Are you in the picture? Isn't the camera broken? Is your heart broken? C'mon, for real? How'd that happen? Do you blame your father? Do you blame your mother? Do you blame God? Aren't you God, though? Are you married? Why? No really, why? What is a contract? Have you ever signed one? About what? What did it ask of you? May I please have this dance? Have you been to Africa? Have you been to Europe? Have you been to Wal-Mart? What did you buy there? How does it taste? Was it genetically modified? How does it feel to drive a car late at night? Do you check the road for cops? Do you check to road for deer? What are you doing driving down an empty road in the middle of the night? Why are you so close to a deer without preparation? Have you memorized your excuse or do you make it up in the moment? Are you in love? Are you in love with yourself? Have you ever worn a uniform? Did it bring you closer to yourself or farther from? Do you work in a uniform? Do your jeans fit perfectly? Do you really like blue jeans? What's your favorite fabric? What's your favorite beverage? Do you know how to swim? Do you know how to fly? Why are you waiting to exhale? Why wait? Why aren't you listening to jazz for at least four hours a day? What are your favorite habits? What do you own? What's yours? Is there a contract? Do you believe in polygamy? The polygraph? The plateau? The great getting up morning that cures the plateau of plurals? Are you satisfied? Have you been boo-ed off the stage at The Apollo? Not even in a dream? Are you boo-ed up? Not even in a dream? Can a question really begin with a knot? Do you like to be tied up or handcuffed during sex? Do you break into hives where the rope was? How often do you cry? Not even in a dream? Do you have a hero? Who's your hero's hero? Who is Thelonious Monk? Who is Eric Dolphy? Who is Sun Ra? Who is Osiris? What is the Ma'at? Who is Ma'at? Have you seen my 42 laws? What is a thyroid? What does it do? What is a third eye? Who is Roy Ayers? Who is Bill Gunn? Who is Kahlil Joseph? What about Mos Def? What's the best place in America? Are you there? Are you on your way? Are you a Marxist? What is an Afro-Harp? Who is Alice Coltrane? Who is Dorothy Ashby? How do you raise your frequency? What's the Big Easy? What's the big idea? Are you an athlete? Are you an entertainer? Aren't you beautiful? Aren't you invisible? Aren't you a great pretender? Is it the iron mask or the Cosby sweater? Guess who's still coming to dinner?

DEAR DAD,

Sometimes I think we confuse re-inventing love with re-inventing death and I think maybe we even like it and need it that way. Maybe we court the kind of confusion that regulates us into our subtler uses, like, you go be the showmanship and I'll be your hippest reason, your once-in-a-resurrection slant rhyme with yourself and helicopter glance/glee, ghetto bird so loud I can finally sleep. It gets paratactic like that like when the sun is up and we get lit. No, the sun is really up. At last. And we lit. Uppity Sun. Up there in that caricature of sky like a lucky number or verse stuck in Rainman's perfect child/mind.

When Amiri died I wept for 2 weeks, off and on, and I keep on shedding some kind of amplitude for him until it feels like he's still here warning me from within *you got to be a spirit, you can't be no ghost,* and *don't ever let anyone break you,* he promised me one night at Blue Note after a Jon Faddis show, before a whisky and Coke. You and Faddis share a birthday, and Jon is O's uncle, it all feels related like a blatant mend in the safest someday, my prince is them.

I was visiting L.A. for the month when it happened, and on my daily, glorious runs among the smog and griffins, spandex and the moonlight's but a spotlight—I wept as I ran and listened to him read under gigantic headphones, and I listened to Theo Parrish and Miles and Amiri reading to me and cried and ran. Sometimes chanting *Witness the Fitness!*

Even mourning feels like a form of vanity in Los Angeles and even realer and rawer for it the way all acts are repetitive and eventually become what they set out to only pretend. But the stranger doesn't even pretend. That's how this year began, like a blunt stranger offering up the weightless baton I've always been waiting to patiently grasp, like its pretense of tumbling into the bluff of me rescued by a sense that enough is not/never enough. It is not. A tainted empathy flailing in the torch that will not stop burning. A new course in tone science, alliances and their obstacles.

You and Amiri were born in the same year and maybe it feels like you've died again, and therefore returned again, and the domain of everything feels clenched in the sudden purgatory between revel and rival (volition and listening), between why now and now's always the time. And I call the fact that I slept with that married guy that same month, that same guy I asked you to help me transcend and banish, I guess I call that a relapse or some kind of reach toward what you and Amiri represent to me but in a new form, trying to replace the heroic with the erotic, failing, triumphantly. And now what? I'm a fugitive? You're a fugitive? It's as if three men died and I could only cry for one. It's as if I am a miracle and I can only perform myself for you and them.

Only the impossible happens. It's as if we're all shepherds in love but mumbling the announcement between sobs and laughter and a deaf flock, not sure which is more accurate of love/at last. We argue over which window to jettison the television from, all those stories below, all told or untold but alive like falling into place, and when it crashes we disagree over which wire caused the burn. In the silence we're left with, I whisper I *hold no grudge* and it sounds like a lie even though it's a lie. Damn. The uncontrollable urge to dance began with standing still in that sounding. And it's the Olympics. I don't watch. It's the limp way competition commits loyalty to satisfy the loyalty it ruins. Hmph. I'm in this beautiful, I've-seen-it-all and nothing at all/is real/are you real?, mood. Miles is still on and all of you have come back to life in me which is difficult like a happy ending with no specific event to call *happy* and endlessly. The happy thing is nowhere to be seen and how safe that has made it. How protected. How reckless. How diligent. How lazy. That dream again.

Today is the day that you give you heart to... Dad, I want you to hold onto your heart now, what if you win your own heart back? Close the door behind those sad cops and come back inside and stay for a while like always. I don't blame you for saving our lives even though some days we forget what to do with them, pagans that we've faithfully been, imagining is remembering. I'm finding more and more that no body knows anything about the Bible anyways. And I think everyone's alive/again. *I had to like, open the bruise up, and let some of the Blues blood come out, to show them.*

It's only love that gets us through,
Harmony

PORTRAIT OF MY FATHER AS A YOUNG MAN

When I was comin' up playin' in the band, I wasn't reading music. I was bullshittin', but I was in the band.

And my father got me an alto out of a pawnshop, and I just picked the motherfucker up, and just started playin' it. And that's the way that went. So he was a musician, he played all the instruments, and all this shit. And my sister, see, she was playing, and I'd get close to her, and pick up on the parts, you know. Playing marches and all that shit.

And then finally my father said, One day, Candice play your part.

I knew god damn well that was my ass, (he knew I wasn't reading). Play your part, Candice.

Now Jimmy play your part. I couldn't read a motherfuckin' note. Not a goddamn note. He said, Get up! (you know he don't curse like I do) Get up and get your fuckin' ass, and work you some scales. Get out.

Now you know my heart was broke. I went and cried, gave a bottle of teardrops. And shit I said, well I'll come back and get these motherfuckers if that's the way they want it.

So I went away and learned how to read the music, still by myself.

I came back in the band, played this music and shit. Cause all that time I was copying on the records, also with the music, so I could fuck these motherfuckers completely up.

So I went in there and they threw the goddamn marches out and I read the music and shit, and everything was great. But what was in my heart... Why all the motherfuckers laughed when they put me out, when I couldn't read, they would come up and say, would you show me how to... play like that.

I'm not gonna show you shit, you rusty motherfucker. So that's the way that went down.

(Imma take my time Imma just try a little, if it don't come out right, fuck it)

HARMONY HOLIDAY is a writer, dancer, and archivist/mythscientist. She lives in New York and Los Angeles.

(CONT'D)

PARTICIPANT	P/W	AFFIL	SHARE
AKOPOFF MIKE	W	BMI	50.00
HOLIDAY JAMES E	W	ASCAP	49.99
EMI UNART CATALOG INC	P	BMI	100.00
UNART-UNART	P	PROCA	.00

TITLE: MAN WITHOUT LOVE   B

PARTICIPANT	P/W	AFFIL	SHARE
HOLIDAY JAMES E	W	ASCAP	99.98
HOUSE OF JOSEPH	P	NA	100.00

TITLE: MEDITERRANEAN SKY   B

PARTICIPANT	P/W	AFFIL	SHARE
SHANNON JACKIE	W	ASCAP	33.33
HOLIDAY JAMES E	W	ASCAP	33.34
MYERS RANDY JAMES	W	ASCAP	33.33
EMI UNART CATALOG INC	P	BMI	100.00
UNART-UNART	P	PROCA	.00

TITLE: MORNING AFTER THE NIGHT BEFORE   B

PARTICIPANT	P/W	AFFIL	SHARE
HOLIDAY JAMES E	W	ASCAP	99.98
EMI UNART CATALOG INC	P	BMI	100.00
UNART-UNART	P	PROCA	.00

TITLE: MOVIN   B

PARTICIPANT	P/W	AFFIL	SHARE

BROADCAST MUSIC INC.
SCHEDULE
HOLIDAY JAMES E   BMI ACCT#   158414
DEPARTMENT: 15   TITLE TYPE: BMI WORK REGISTRATION

DATE: 04/08/200
PAGE: 18

P/W	AFFIL	SHARE
W	BMI	50.00
W	ASCAP	49.99
P	MI	00.00
P	OCA	0

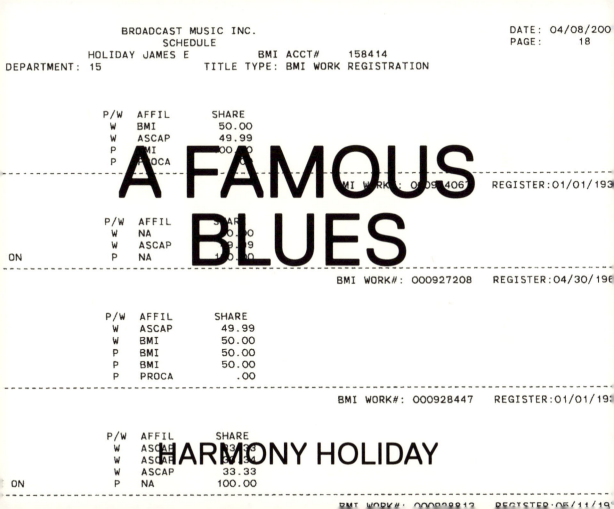

BMI WORK#: 000 406 REGISTER: 01/01/193

P/W	AFFIL	SHARE
W	NA	50.00
W	ASCAP	9.19
P	NA	100.00

ON

BMI WORK#: 000927208 REGISTER: 04/30/196

P/W	AFFIL	SHARE
W	ASCAP	49.99
W	BMI	50.00
P	BMI	50.00
P	BMI	50.00
P	PROCA	.00

BMI WORK#: 000928447 REGISTER: 01/01/193

P/W	AFFIL	SHARE
W	ASCAP	33.33
W	ASCAP	33.34
W	ASCAP	33.33
P	NA	100.00

ON

BMI WORK#: 000928813 REGISTER: 05/11/19

(CONT'D)

PARTICIPANT
DAVIS MAC (ACCT
HOLIDAY JAMES E
EMI UNART CATALO
UNART-UNART

TITLE: LOVE ON TOP OF T

PARTICIPANT
COHEN MURRAY
HOLIDAY JAMES E
WRITER CLEARANCE

TITLE: LOVE THE TIME IS

PARTICIPANT
HOLIDAY JAMES E
WOMACK BOBBY
ABKCO MUSIC INC
EMI UNART CATALO
UNART-UNART

TITLE: LOVE WILL FIND A

PARTICIPANT
SHANNON JACKIE
HOLIDAY JAMES E
MYERS RANDY JAME
WRITER CLEARANCE

TITLE: LOVE WON T LIVE

ON *GO FIND YOUR FATHER / A FAMOUS BLUES*

Do any black children grow up casual? Naw, we grow up shipped, knowing that we are loved but knowing more than that, that terror, that knowing is scrawled money for our bank. We're sure-shot and avoided, singing blue devil blues like a black and blue disciple, out from Sallis, Attala off delta, change-played, flowed to that subcommon up-river fate, our Waterloo and phonic quarry, step-sharp, sharp-squared, strait-shawled, boot-sharp visitor, made for walking, talking remnant of an extra-impossible accord, then Los Angeles. Resonances and renascence of everywhere we come from, Harmony, deepest Holiday since Jason, since Jimmy, having gone to find him, makes these missive runs, assured of her allure but running from and in that into open, unsure dream. She sees it's getting late. Her archive has a microtonal blush. Sightsound, as Russell Atkins says. Can you say what it is to sing a song of love I can show you, right here, ask me now.

— FRED MOTEN

13 BLUES/13 WAYS OF BEING YOUR IMMORTALITY

The Black Entertainer's Slow Memory Blues (The imagination as a form of memory) (imagining is remembering) (what's entertainment?) (Hero auditions) (Interviews Transcribed from Memory)

The Quit Copying me Blues (keep copying me and Imma —The empty threat blues) (the sellout blues) (villain auditions) (molecular revolution)

(everybody wannabe a nigga but nobody wanna *be* a nigga)

The *Nigga are you Black* Blues (Imitative Magic)
The Black Entertainer's Unknown Blues (I don't know that man) (who dat is) (know who you is know who you ain't) (nigga you ain't anonymous) (synonyms and heteronyms)

The Black Entertainer's I'm *God* Blues (what I'm trying to say is you're a slave) (the three stages of pimping—main stage) (Polytheism for geniuses)

The *What's My Name* Blues (Polyandry for geniuses) (Moods in Free Time) (Victory and Sorrow)

Lament for the Brilliance of Wolves (Appear surreal) (You're nothing but a savior) (Guns and Change)

The Half-Hearted Blues (as a robot gets herself together)

The Black and Tan Fantasy Blues (I'll be your mirror)   **The Missing Myth Blues** (Show me your myths) (the misplaced myth blues)

(is she your mistress too) (the *music is my mistress* blues)
(light bright/light blue hue)

The Curious Yellow Blues (Music for Chameleons) **The Famous Blues** (cause that's what niggas do)

(Why I am a destiny)

The Black and Immortal Blues (stayin' alive) (don't stay in a lie) (I'll stay, he'll be comin' back) (wait, what?) (*Shhhhhh, Peaceful*)

ROCKET
APROACHING
OUTER SPACE

A BLACK ENTERTAINER'S SLOW MEMORY BLUES

Heroes are so rare it's you or no one. It may have been better to have stayed out there in the country and planted olive trees, had a lot of children and beaten your wife, do you still love to sing?

TITLE: HE'LL NEVER GROW OLD   BMI

PARTICIPANT	P/W	AFFIL	SHARE
HOLIDAY JAMES E	W	ASCAP	99.98
EMI UNART CATALOG INC	P	BMI	100.00
UNART UNART	P	PROCA	.00

TITLE: HE'S ALL I NEED   BMI

AKA: SHE'S ALL I NEED

(MORE...)

COMPOSER-SINGER JIMMY HOLIDAY DIES

AP, Associated Press

Feb. 19, 1987 8:46 PM ET

WATERLOO, IOWA WATERLOO, Iowa (AP) _ James "Jimmy" Holiday, who composed songs for such artists as Sonny and Cher, Ray Charles and The Staple Singers, has died at age 52.

Holiday died of heart failure Sunday at University Hospitals in Iowa City.

His songs have been recorded by Ray Charles, Glen Campbell, Jackie DeShannon, The Staple Singers, Sonny and Cher, Mac Davis, Sam Cooke, Kenny Rogers, Dottie West and others.

He wrote "All I Ever Need is you," recorded by Sonny and Cher; "Put a Little Love in Your Heart," by Jackie DeShannon; "Hey Mister," by Ray Charles; "God Bless the Children," by The Staple Singers; and "The Girls of Texas," by Ry Cooder.

He was born July 24, 1934, in Sallis, Miss., and grew up in Waterloo.

He was a self-employed singer and composer before retiring from singing in 1969, but he continued to compose until the time of his death.

Holiday combined Charles' musical style with his own and credited the late Sam Cooke with teaching him music writing skills.

Burial was scheduled for Friday in Waterloo.

THE NIGGA ARE YOU BLACK? BLUES / SWEET DOUBLE HIPNESS

This sense of duality is really key to delusion

Was your father a hero too?

I mean was your father a singer too?

Was your father cool too? Cruel too?

This sense of duality is really key   to delusion

Was your father black too, I mean, blue-black like a heroine habit tied to you and so unlimited

you could just burst about it? Geyser and shout to a disappearing lord/such a disappearing lord, was your father disappearing too? And here too? Where to? Did he come true like a dream? Or hang on like a fantasy or primal/scream. *In Heaven's name, why do we play these games.* If he didn't beat you, did he at least join you? Where do you get your ideas from? Is it true that imagining is remembering? Imagining is remembering.

It's true.

That time I saw him stealing chickens from the tender heads of goats grew prominent, celebrant, token mystic, elaborate, bratty, ashy-to-classy, whatever—never tentative. And how he turned them into resilient tropes for how close to say *I love you* to a white woman until she turns you yellow and all will and owl. He was a genius. I'm in his cirine/proof. Poof, I'm in her. I'm here. I'm here. Amber blur on the white man's burden. The softest nose on the hill and the truest eyes, wrists the size of the word *copper* inside of cool velvet. If I have to, I fight my way into the beautiful songs, but mostly there are no rivals for a whole double album about his blunt reappraisal of birds he sat behind recording glass pressing his throat against the nappy/kinky/tight-curled-afro/southern silence until they felt their names were blind and whole enough to invent time and hide it (hide your time!), fractured enough to be suture and ax in the same lunging (no this ain't the jungle) stillness —black enough to call the sun blue as it disappears into the sound.

Between you and me,

I think every man is impersonating his mother, from the first time he saw her get free on a drug or duty, to the time he watched her get new on time, he sings to her from his hinter mind, wait for me, wait for me. Some of them are just better at it. The tyrants and infants and their perfect daughters, perfectly happy and *not* lost. Don't be so miscellaneous, give your note a name, he said, palms covered in feathers, radio speakers on his shoulder, Sam Cooke blowing through them, and then a commercial for sleeping/pills.

Is your father sleeping too?

An eternal higher principal, of pure light, has been turned against the earlier, fluctuating principal of

both darkness and light, death and resurrection, the sun against the moon. The sun never dies. The sun descends into the netherworld, battles demons of the night sea, is in danger, but never, dies. And the inhabiting spirit of this mythology is wonder. No such rambling as the hill. A black bull miraculously engendered by a moonbeam, gleaming, gleaming, gleaming, learning the gangster lean, the high yellow tusk clean as a solo violin coming through a corvette radio onto the black ballerina's lap—of sun. Some sin. Aftermath. Post-math. Pre-black/habit. Ancient to the future—

What truth is coming through your father that is going to come through you.   What soldier's dream is so true it has to die for you? Is your father god too? Lied to by the good book. Are you god too? Blood on the leaves, blood at the roots. Groupies by the speaker vibrating and mouthing the

lyrics, Am I blue,   you'd be too?
        Picture it.
Is that your father in the picture too Blue altitude in his muse I be I miss you I miss you too

At least we win the movie To the race industry in crisis what do we win? Mellow hype?
                        Mellow hype.

As a robot gets herself together, and we do it, and we get to the middle, where we have forgotten our feelings of love, you will help me, huh?

THE BLACK ENTERTAINER'S QUIT COPYING ME BLUES

No for real, quit copying me.

No for real, quit copying me. (echo like a ghetto breeze in the suburbs you can't help but trust and follow-follow all the way to us and so

I'm practicing the making of the sound I into a vacuum and out comes swoon

I said quit copying me

Okay? Ok. (*Ofay loving nigga*, she mumbles, squeezing his hand   like a pencil or penicillin or pendulum or peninsula, son, three-sided dream come true in the 5th dimension:

Great it passes on

Passing on, it becomes remote

Having become remote, it returns.

What you will know of me is the shadow of the arrow that has hit its target. To remake myself and remake you, I return to my state of garden and shadow, code and tone, cool reality and the well-lit fantasy that sells as what you think you know of me or all you wish you'd stolen, ship after ship after—and the a cappella version of Tupac's Black Cotton over James Brown's Big Payback over Amiri's Mass Angel Costume. Few people know my whole name, he shouted, from your mouth. Your

insolence must be kept in bounds by dignity, but your dignity's gotta be soul, ruthlessly. Isn't history obnoxious compared to our best intentions. Didn't we posse up like we meant business and march right in on the pleasure principal like I place my cheek on the suede of his drum and that's where this speech comes from

Not another pilgrim.
      Not Guilt
Not another wounded angel, but a magnetic person
            Not another gun in your mouth where I belong
            Get it together man, fumble for the switch
            Together we're making cartwheels and some reeling shadow wants to cloak the fringe and innit
Why I'm you're hero
Natural
Immortal
Great   day in the morning   knack for recognizing   when   Indignation is a prison
and escaping it with refuge wit   We hide   the word indigenous in the Dozens, once we dig it
up. *Yo momma's so indigenous the only English she speaks is singing* There she is with Jesus telling him to quit
copying her while he bleeds through the cross and lives forever—pentamorphic, pentatonic, Yoruba,
blues-strutting-so-what-mythscientist   and never makes the top ten softest rappers in the game list
And when he's highest he testifies   *I'll admit   that was costume gravity, but it lifted us, up*

Under the U.S. copyright law, as amended by the Sound Recording Act of 1971, a copyright is granted in a sound recording separate and apart from the copyright granted in the underlying song. Copyright ownership vests in the person who actually creates or writes a given work of authorship the moment the expression is "fixed in a tangible medium". In the case of a songwriter that would be when the song is written down or recorded; in the case of a recording artist that would be when the master is recorded by the artist. If the work is created as a "work made for hire", however, then the company who hires or employs the artist is the author of the work and owns all rights in the work for copyright purposes.

Record contracts are structured as ongoing recording commitments where the label agrees to pay for the production of one album with options to require additional albums from the artist at their discretion. The record label pays an advance to the artist for the cost of producing the album and the artist then records and delivers the album to the record label on a work made for hire basis. The record company agrees to pay the artist a royalty on any sales of the album based on an extremely complex calculation involving numerous variables (subject to recoupment of any and all advances from the artist's royalty).

The dilemma for the artist is that, although the artist pays for the cost of producing an album, the record company owns the album as an asset and, since most of the advance is used to pay for recording costs, the artist ends up with very little money in his or her pocket. Since the record label can cross-collateralize unrecouped advances from one album against royalties payable from any other album, the artist could conceivably sell a great many albums and still be in an unrecouped position with its record label - and while the artist remains in an unrecouped position, the record company is making a profit on each album sold.

THE BLACK ENTERTAINER'S UNKNOWN BLUES

I don't know that man. Je ne connais pas cet homme. Who dat is? That that nigga André? Nah, I don't know him. Does he sing? Rap? Play Jazz? Blues? Quote H. Rapp Brown on tape? Any felonies? How many kids? How many moms? Fuck it. *Let that nigga in.*

But I was thinking about the gun in your mouth/that time. How you placed it there like a logo or a lie that won't let go or how a quarantined idea turns into a demon which just means hidden thing and how if I just expose the thing it becomes its own answer/it becomes its own father with its own weapon turned on himself.

        And the reckoning is now in mythological, not earthly, terms. And violence becomes part of our expressive continuum. Inevitable, valuable, and then invisible when we heal like the trouble
        with all this healing is that the scar is us. We meet again,
anyways/innocence.

Love was a weapon then and the song went up in camels and made us millions. In the first room there was the second, in second room there was the third. There are seven rooms in her, at least, each one a man she loves, he leaves, her name alone is worth a fortune and,

Do any black children grow up casual?

And that other time after we got car jacked in L.A. on the way home from Spago. Like a scene outta that movie I don't like about those hoes I don't love. It is hard out there for a pimp. A white woman and her brown babies/brown babies in a fancy car with unlocked doors. Most everything is semi-automatic. Two black men hopped into the front row seats and started waving guns like pom-poms. *We made it! We made it!* Right against the rim of her porcelain brain. All they wanted was the car and the color. The car was white like her. She saved our lives. Then the penguins came over with a book full of photos of black men, so serious like kings in their mugging, and they asked us to pick which two it had been. I was five but I could feel the shrugged evil of it so true and impossible to touch as I pretended to recognize us. We closed our eyes and pointed at you, and said, *I don't know that man. Je ne connais pas cet homme.* We saved our lives. We tugged at the flashlight looking for bruises and found you awake, and found a way.

17

YOUR MOTHER AND FATHER,
SAT. 11/23/86
OR GIVEING YOU A-
DAY OF MUSIC
INJOY YOURSELF MUCH LOVE
ALWAYS-SO-HUMON

GIRL HUMON

AND KNOW THAT WE
LOVE YOU yes WE LOVE YOU.

PARTICIPANT	P/W	AFFIL	SHARE
HOLIDAY JAMES E	W	ASCAP	99.98
EMI UNART CATALOG INC	P	BMI	100.00
UNART-UNART	P	PROCA	.00

TITLE: HEAD OVER HEELS IN...

PARTICIPANT	P/W	AFFIL	SHARE
HOLIDAY JAMES E	W	ASCAP	99.98
EMI UNART CATALOG INC	P	BMI	100.00
UNART-UNART	P	PROCA	.00

TITLE: HEAVENLY ANGEL

PARTICIPANT	P/W	AFFIL	SHARE
INO FLOYD	W	BMI	50.00
HOLIDAY JAMES E	W	ASCAP	49.99
FORESIDE PUBLISHING COMPANY	P	NA	

TITLE: HIDDEN TEARS

PARTICIPANT	P/W	AFFIL	SHARE
COBB GARY	W	NA	50.00
HOLIDAY JAMES E	W	ASCAP	49.99
CIMARRON MUSIC CO	P		100.00

TITLE: HIGH SCHOOL

PARTICIPANT	P/W	AFFIL	SHARE
BOLTON MELE	W	ASCAP	
HOLIDAY JAMES E	W	ASCAP	25.00
LAWS TROY	W	ASCAP	25.00
WOMACK FRIENDLY	W	BMI	25.00
DERGLENN MUSIC	P	BMI	25.00
OLD BROMPTON ROAD PUBLISHING	P	ASCAP	75.00

18

THE BLACK ENTERTAINER'S SAY MY NAME BLUES

You know how when the sun is out 'til really late one day every year and he renames your soul to pace while you play Apollo shoulders with your first born self and everyone feels like a nearness/ winner/narcissist/ridiculous/*charmed-I'm-sure*-chanting miss thing chasing her shadow beneath that yellow umbrella where the slow word for mirror rears itself to roar and before you can dwell on it or rest assured or aurora that staggered velocity, his love for you, your lust for the father, you're busy *combating it all not so fast with your fat tongue all over my name like a claw or a bad actor as I shine on the grass in your mouth and you get how*—Love is a dangerous necessity. Is this man imitating a movie star? In another quarantine of lights. Atum-Ra. Oatmeal Man. Watermelon Man. Simple. Charlie. Blues for Mister Charlie. Deacon. Emperor. Drummer immersed in soar and sunlore. *And he has no sons to float in the space between.* Husband. Has been. Atum-Ra. One mo' gin. What dat is? That that nigga André? Does he have the miracles with him? The mirages? The Tupac Hologram? The fix? *Crucifix* to you. Cruise with it. And we do. Do-rag situated on the climb like a crown by now   like a stammering arrow on the way to rose

And I'm moving forward toward my myth so fluent it's catatonic—some blues but not the kind that's trauma, the kind when you're not afraid enough to make satisfaction taboo yet the narcissism of small differences still huddles around the question like a *gimme* or a bright gimmick at the lost gates, and interrogates: I want to know if you are single or married, how you live, if you're still a slave—

The typical illusion is that it feels black to be black, 8 bars and a plastic heart/surgeon later, a prayer to the surge, *you are my starship, you are my starship,* what color is this blaze?

Beginning in 2013, rights of certain songs can revert to the original artist, meaning they'll get all future royalties instead of the record label they originally signed with. The one big exception is if the song is a "work for hire" - commissioned by an organization and not the independent work of another party. (This is an overly simplified explanation but hopefully you get the point.) Sadly for artists, record labels have fraudulently declared many songs as "works for hire" allowing the labels to keep ownership. Artists in this category will be screwed forever.

For technical legal reasons this is at issue in the upcoming MP3tunes trial, but there are implications for ALL artists. If this incorrect designation holds up, then these artists will never get ownership and the future royalties that comes along with it. In the MP3tunes case we have chance to get a ruling that these works are NOT works for hire, paving the way for these works to be returned to the artist without a multi-year battle which will likely cost millions (since MP3tunes has already gone through much of this).

What I'm looking for is an artist who has the courage to stand up on this issue and claim their works, laying the groundwork for them and ALL artists who share their plight to take ownership in the near future and escape this slavery. (Rather like Curt Flood did battling to get free agency for baseball players: See The Curious Case of Curt Flood which should have been called the Courage Case of Curt Flood.)

Below is a list of artists that EMI is trying to claim perpetual licenses of their works. It is not a complete list of artists that are screwed forever and these are only artists signed to EMI. (Other labels have engaged in the same unscrupulous behavior.) If you know any of these artists or managers or legal representation,

THE BLACK ENTERTAINER'S I'M GOD BLUES

en for some, the anxiety becomes charisma. You know you've been spoiled like a dalmatian/hysteria/numb, nigga playing god
n m/term/faith/culture/affirmation/ature to give or even rather the tiny eternity of a chasm where fame and anonymity shadow
inc……………………… e tangle from django to shango, Griot, growl, row of
ut one treehouse on the perch to signal purchase or that those roving eyes are to scale or for sale and forever. My map to the
orld is through the foot which was the drum in the field which trusts the run/don't kneel/ to mean, to me, to medium —
ce, which these days is about disappearing and in the film I'm making it's a black entertainer's main thing, remember

ards, lack words, excess words, words that are dance words that beat me to it **He was a maniac? Did we notice that?** ds that beat me to it words I beat you with or for ——— **Gods were never decent**
father words or for example, just 8 lettered minutes of montage of black men and women running, from the cops, from their
t, from their wives, from their husbands, from their mistresses, from their masters, and re-masters, from their children, from the
ssions, from their triumphs, from the sun gods, from the humming neon of progress and slow change, from the gold chain, from
ld medal, from the training, from the narcissism of differences small and large, in the rain, from the rain, to the rain, tainted

h **What I'm trying to say is that you're a slave** where it all converges, a spotlight with no one in it and do you get
ignant or make a subtle shift in pitch to reach the place that's neither ironic nor overly-earnest which is where the imagination
us real to ourselves on either side of time and space/intangible and certain and chimes jingling in the race toward nirvana
s invisible camels calm as a blues echo in the footsteps of **And that means you're nothing** gh of our survival **but a savior**
ut of no where—

LAMENT FOR THE BRILLIANCE OF WOLVES

Abbey Lincoln, Oshun, Ma-'at, Shakti, Sade, Ai, Badu, Ruby Dee, James Baldwin, Jimmy Holiday, Nina Simone, Harmony, Clarice Lispector, Brother Weldon, Phylicia Rashad, The eternal triangle, the ghetto oracle, Sonia Sanchez, Bill Gunn, Amiri Baraka, Wilson Harris, what truth is coming through your father that is going to come through you? David Bowie, Janet Jackson, Betty Mabry aka Betty Davis, Francis Davis, Miles Away/ke, cakewalk, raw cakes, Cicely Tyson, Alice Coltrane, what truth is coming through your mother that is going to come through you? John Coltrane, Ornette Coleman, Trayvon Martin, Prince, Beyoncé, Michael Jackson, Helene Johnson, Dorothy Dandridge, Jackie McLean, Jackie Robinson, Marvin Gaye, Frank Ocean, Billie Holiday, Dionysus, James Baldwin, James Baldwin, James Baldwin, James Baldwin, your mom, yo momma, your yo-yo, your you, and your man—

lament for the killing of wolves
for the shooting of wolves
for the surveillance of wolves by helicopter

for their rebellion

for the young rebels in cubic packs gentrified by lament

for the song they stack into psalm

salty in the honest air

nestled between terror and tom-toms, fearless, careless, peerless, us,

it/ain't necessarily so, it ain't so bad   to be addicted to the myth   where dialog is a home and we

paid the cost to be the boss of it and

I still love you so much more   than what's happening

more than Good Times, more than The Cosby Show, more than BET, more than neat corn rows that
pull the sorrow from eyes and I abide, rejoicing, rejoicing   a little paranoid, a little paranormal
decoy type   in dark shades mumbling   *you ain't seen me, right?*   Then taking to the stage in my next
disguise to accept his Grammy in *gimme* grammar, mercenary and phantom

IVAN HOFFMAN, B.A., J.D.
Attorney At Law

Internet and Intellectual Property Law

10736 Jefferson Blvd.
#436
Culver City, CA 90230-4933
(310) 600-9179
e-Fax: (208) 545-0558
emailivan@ivanhoffman.com
https://www.ivanhoffman.com
Leveraging With Integrity™

February 17, 2009

Mr. Tony Akyer
Davis, Shapiro, Lewit & Hayes, LLP
193 South Rodeo Drive
Suite 200
Beverly Hills, CA 90212

RE: Tangerine Music and Racer Music/Jimmy Holiday

Dear Mr. Akyer:

On behalf of my clients, The Ray Charles Foundation including its publishing divisions, Tangerine Music and Racer Music, enclosed please find a number of royalty statements. When you approve the same my clients will issue one check payable to Piere III, LLC and send that check to your office per the terms of your letter of direction dated October 21, 2008.

The statements are for the period ended June 30, 2004 through December 31, 2008. See explanation below.

The compositions published by Tangerine Music and Racer Music written or co-written by Jimmy Holiday are as set forth below. My clients intend to cooperate with you and your clients to arrange a transfer of the renewal period rights to the same but only as to the Jimmy Holiday share of such compositions and as otherwise set forth below. You should prepare the appropriate paperwork and submit the same to me for review. In any situation in which my clients retain rights to a composition, administration by Tangerine or Racer or your clients' company or designee would, accordingly, be on a non-exclusive basis. Since this make us for a difficult licensing situation, you may wish to consider allowing Tangerine to retain exclusive administration rights.

Peace of Mind

Co-Written by Holiday and Ray Charles. Therefore, you will have to prepare, makes to The Harry Fox Agency and BMI that Tangerine now only administers 1/2 of the publisher's share.

PARTICIPANT   HOLIDAY JAMES E   LIGOI
DANIEL JESSIE
PARTICIPANT   P/W AFFIL   SHARE
   W   NA   33.33
   W   ASCAP   33.34

Being Young

Written by Holiday. Therefore, you will have to prepare notices to The Harry Fox Agency and BMI that Tangerine no longer administers this composition.

All Of My Life

Co-Written by Holiday and Ray Charles. Therefore, you will have to prepare notices to The Harry Fox Agency and BMI that Tangerine now only administers 1/2 of the publisher's share.

I've Got To Make It.

Co-Written by Holiday and Mike Akapoff. Therefore, you will have to prepare notices to The Harry Fox Agency and BMI that Tangerine now only administers 1/2 of the publisher's share.

I'm Not Crying

Co-written by Holiday and Charles Underwood and co-published by Tangerine and Underwood Music. It is unclear whether Tangerine or Underwood Music was the original publisher since the contracts are uncertain. Accordingly, Tangerine is unable to convey any renewal rights to this composition at this time and you will have to straighten this out with Underwood Music.

her writes you letters in fat crayola waxes and they've been kept in the mirror sill like so
to suddenly know it. And to create the feeling of exchange without the loneliness of
, would you learn to write yourself those letters now that your father's have gone missing,
t them on purpose because there's something you've been meaning to tell yourself and he
And what part of you would these letters become to come from. Would they be more like

THE BLACK ENTERTAINER'S HALF-HEARTED BLUES

that's that plan, do you only know
intimate. And how would they begin... Dear lucky one, dear daydreamer, I learn so much
these days, about how to play the blues, so economical and so spare and yet so right.

It's really very very real to be here tonight in relation to life and death and I'm sure they both love each other

yourself and lion to yourself, a cannibal all mellow like in the emerald green but showing
no camouflage, star spangled smoke, and how it's become so advanced that you have
say at the beginnings of conversations. You choose to say nothing. Hello your quietness.

And only love has saved each revelation from the madness of opinions, only love can do that.

, dear what we think we kno
avior. What if we decided to begin all meetings with a few moments of silence. Not too
enough timelessness to remind us what's important about being there. I bet it'd be
ng and centering like a Trane song, The Drum Thing, so satisfying it makes all else feel
d now it's the most effective way to hide or show or so loud it can't be heard. Dear spirit
r unbridled love. I love wanted the pretty beauty and the ugly beauty to go between

As a robot gets herself together

er seamlessly and share the audience and the dream and the feeling of loss and
ness that gives us our memory of the dream in pieces of mirror corner that lean out at us

(How does this love bring life and death together, tell me.)

t the day like slang, like a grammar we mangle to earth. Even Cecil Dolphy, dear
ar shelter of your parent arms... save your father's words, that's what you've been meaning
rself, don't be afraid to save them... We won't need a plot, we'll go deep enough into
we won't need a plot. You are a soldier of good fortune. You are a maverick in a world of
most everyone wants to be theatrical, and it's so thrilling to me, that you don't fake it

That's A Lie

Co-Written by Holiday and Ray Charles. Therefore, you will have to prepare notices to The Harry Fox Agency and BMI that Tangerine now only administers 1/2 of the publisher's share.

Will I Ever Get Home

Co-Written by Holiday and Ray Charles. Therefore, you will have to prepare notices to The Harry Fox Agency and BMI that Tangerine now only administers 1/2 of the publisher's share.

The compositions below are those owned or administered by Racer Music.

Something Inside Me

Written by Holiday and co-published by Versil Music. Apparently the deal was that Versil signed the original copyright agreement with Holiday and then assigned 1/2 the copyright to Racer with the provision that Racer pay the writer and Versil. So it appears that Versil is the one who lost the renewal rights. Accordingly, Racer is

THE BLACK AND TAN FANTASY BLUES

And you feel like an occupied territory screaming *change!, father, change!* I'll admit I'm yearning to be one of the rare cases where a man's most famous song is also his best, to appear surreal and effortlessly real in the same headtrip—there. I said it. Don't get in my superstition or you'll end up hidden, like Bigger, he knows the deal.

Bigger is my *shhhhh, justice.*

Bigger is my hoodrich telepath in a rigorous woods I don't dare ~~took~~ enter

An introduction to non-fascist life begins with hymn null and penitent frontiers for him from here to the hook to the distant lover—*as a robot gets herself together and we do it, and we get the middle, where we have forgotten our feelings of love, you will helpme, huh?*

But he's out looking for Black Aphrodite (as depicted by a white actress in the film about her life)

And I feel like an occupied territory screaming *change!, nigga, change!*

TITLE: EVERYBODY NEEDS SOMEBODY
PARTICIPANT
HOLIDAY JAMES E
UNART UNA
TITLE: EVERYTHING IS LOVE
PARTICIPANT
EMI UNART CATALOG INC
UNART-UNART
TITLE: FINDER S KEEPERS LOSERS WEEP
PARTICIPANT
CHAMBERS CLIFF
HOLIDAY JAMES E
LEWIS JAMES E
WRITER CLEARANCE FOR DELETE
TITLE: FOR HER LOVE

And then when he did, the reforms annoyed me

He became too common to tame the ongoing carapace of irony/we both know about how we both know about it but being cryptic is really pretty nauseating so, quick! Picture Richard Pryor singing *My Old Flame* to a room full of newborns on a rainy cruise ship under pulsating cameras that rub the tears off his cold sweat, as shields, and we get better and better. And we be healed to invisible

As a robot gets herself together and we do it—

There is a space where you thought you would be, but which you refuse to grab hold of. You save his life every day. You love that space

THE MISSING MYTH BLUES / *MY ARCHIVES, YOUR ARCHIVES, OUR ARCHIVES*

The scandal is leaving; the scandal is changing hands, approving of itself, more and more ramps, more and more answers for the bland delirium of restraint—

                                        Are you addicted to chaos too?

                        It hurts to stop there, so early in the mentality we still remember how to parody healing with appropriateness like 2.5 cars/kids, and suddenly is gradual, and chaos is impossible but we shout *Nigga this goes out to chaos* into the cloak of our leap

            from ourselves   to ourselves again

And now you know me well enough to betray me and

The meaning of a man   can lilt and dream and get a little voluptuous   and mink   and willing
You're my thrill you're a killer you're an angel you're no where   you're so black I can't even see you smiling in the spotlight   (that's a joke, you can laugh)   There you are, head back behind a kiss, laughing   it off   the tempo like temptation, temptation
                        And they say it's a black thing, promising magic replicas from imaging them as

such   All the choreographer said was, *don't act demure*, and as if your torso is shredding, and at the heart of any disassembly, a reunion

And you can become real like me. Five easy payments of 29.95 and an eternity of denial lets me inherit the real thing from its hidden place on the record and loop it and be prepared
As a robot gets herself together, and we do it, and we get to the part where we have forgotten our feelings for love, you will helpme, huh?

MONEY FOR
YOUR BANK

BE GOOD

HARMONY HOLIDAY
FROM YOUR MOTHER
FATHER
WITH MUCH LOVE

JIMMY HOLIDAY

A FAMOUS BLUES

Thelonious, Thelonious Sphere, Born 1934 Sallis, Mississippi It appears you're famous, Thelonious.

That's what that mean? You get famous and they put your name in—in that book? Hmmm, I'm famous, ain't that a bitch!

(The heart swells with suppressed excitement)

He knows it's toxic; knows it's the opposite of sane, to find home base in the spotlight, all your
thoughts slicing into his name like soggy matches rubbing a fiend, for prices

*I practice most when I'm loaded/ I'm gonna get that nectar, and I'm gonna leave—some inventory for next time/ Shoulder fruit, 8
rings minus the suffering/*
*Can you tell me what they said to my father that made him go numb, go to church, obey the draft whispered onto his torment, and
what they'll say to us/ You'll be pulled away from your post of surveillance on that day/ It's not the protection from death we ever
need, we rotate, we prefer to be safe from your forms*

So if you think about me, and you ain't gonna do no revolutionary act, forget about me, I don't want myself on your mind

34

THE CURIOUS YELLOW BLUES / MUSIC FOR CHAMELEONS Welcome to Violence

You punch in the face and red flowers bloom.

Like lashes on a dark back bulging into swoon, and we're supposed to feel actual and whole to that living myth in your mouth spilling out as blood and howl; that rubaiyat, that double bolted hipness, and just rollick in it. Cool, we did. I promise. To remain as promiscuous as this very moment and as hard to please too. I won't let its beauty make me lazy. I felt the disorientation of sweet violence and became drunk with it and ate so much gold I witnessed the eternal sphinx smiling through his lie into the glistening cowardice of a caged lion-like, and lunged right into my iron limbs, my wonder streak, my glass crease of attitude and tease and aloof and *do you know who I am*—made them into a griot family, entreating, *members don't get weary, members don't get weary*. Treat me how you hear me. Do you hear me? Are we here/now? Neither black nor white, a ripe golden rum colored (not that it mattered) aristocrat, stallion, item, totem, something else. Most people. Are ashamed of their fascination, is all. I don't blame them for how loud and shapeless the privacy gets before it ruptures and turns a race.

And these days. These days I feel like a motherless child, falling in love with father, brave enough—
brave enough for anything but
silence

THE BLACK AND IMMORTAL BLUES / 4 NIGGAS (ONLY)?

Did you see him? That Black man running backwards in the rain? A suspect? An aspect. 360 respect/ spectator shouting *Get your Africa tickets! Get your Africa Tickets!*—Into the black maybe or *Maybe your baby done made some other plans. With some other man*—Out the taxi window—Immortal or not, he felt so superfluous in the west wind like earth rot in search of lotus and sometimes the opposite, like beauty so tender it shatters when you look to it, an innervision, and intervention. *As a robot gets herself together, and we do it, and we get to the middle, where we have forgotten our feelings of love, you will helpme, huh?*

Well, clap dammit! I'm serious. I cannot believe the conditions that produced a situation that demanded a man like this, or a song like this.

But I love tomorrow as much as the next ritual or quiet letter to a brink or robot singing/*nothing more than feelings*, a particularly candid accomplishment, an abundance we borrowed from shame, *sing!, nigga, sing!*, I can hear you thinking blue and root and who are you this lifetime and did you find your father, finally, and part the obsession into neat braids—Rapunzel with a rapper fetish—It becomes increasingly difficult to find where jazz starts and where jazz ends, I think, pretty soon.

And anyway I don't believe in freedom. I don't think anything like that exists,

in the world or in music. I think there are higher laws, though, and when you move under higher laws you operate under fewer laws thus moving into a state of relative freedom compared to being under numerous, smaller laws. What is that nigga running from, anyways?

HIS NAME IS SLIM He isn't dead. He isn't a dead poet of rhythm. He shook the locals like a passing train, coal-coal/now-now nameless then militant, like an underneath, like combed out math, to clone an oath, I *do*/I *do*, and he kept on living. Some say, forever. Forever and sunsmell/happily ever, Osiris-ever—ever hear him laugh? Some say the swell of rain around an averted catastrophe/like fame in the knees and speechless, blue's pain, and none too provincial, how the nails of courage drill into the mercenary air. He's a leanless pimp, alive of it, and a pimp without a lean could become president, as the old saying stays. Oh let it not become clever or clutter or clique or oar or riddle or order, this borderless, borderline pchizo grip of his go getting. Let it work like a babbling clock in a movie scene, mending the risk with dash and fiction. He isn't dead. She's on blast/duty screaming daddy into the mirror until it glows with her. When did *nigga* become our favorite word(k)/But be sure of it, that he's the sublime puzzle, the rough cheer approaching us as spell. Why are you so dark, nigga, why you so dark and soldier near.

Her name is Sweet Thing

HIS NAME IS MALIK

He beats his wife and preaches about the revolution and an invisible mineral he calls *consciousness* to sold out auditoriums. Quotes Duke Ellington's *A Drum Is a Woman* in cliché smoke-laden dressing room conversations, all vertical and vertigo, with his boys after speeches. Love is a dangerous necessity (again). Groupies peek in with crisp, eager eyes. He squeezes my hand a little tighter like a thigh afterhours. Take out the part where he beats his wife. Add a magic/cactus cutting masks for light. He's a revolutionary. Can't you see. He's why I tell my story fast. He's why I'm your hero. He's where beauty goes to keep. He's not just a rapper, he's just a robot. As a robot gets himself together, and he does it, and he gets the middle where we have forgotten our feelings of love you will helphim, huh?

Her name is Saffronia
Her name is Saffronyella

TYLM281   BROADCAST MUS
SHORT CAT   SCHEDUL
CATALOG COUNT: 171   HOLIDAY JAMES E
REQUESTED BY: JEREMY COHEN   DEPARTMENT: 15   T

(CONT'D)
                    PARTICIPANT   P/W   AFFIL
                    HOLIDAY JAMES E   W   ASCAP
                    LEWIS JAMES E   W   BMI
                    EMI UNART CATALOG INC   P   BMI

HIS NAME IS LEROY

A clean black man in a numb Cadillac, driving down the rent. He doesn't believe in memory. He leans against auburn bricks like a slave or Elvis and tells his story to pray for us in 4/4 to infinity. He takes the great black superlative and turns it into a toy soldier which he knocks off of a manmade cliff in the suburbs, where it floats forever—on, calm like a balloon animal hugging the bulk of his infatuation so desperately/reckless, it's suave. Good things are *solid!* Better things are *out of this world!* He believes that exile is the cure for exile. He's all soul-less style; he leaves his body before you can kick him out. On the other side of the game he makes a commercial for the next black superlative and becomes Spike Lee, someone to love and lead and blame for love, and leave. Race rant scene. Blank screen. Love scene. Love is an eager necessity. You call him a sellout, you steal his woman, you train his suntan pale. He smiles, finds a new woman with a hipper nose and all yellow/the vogue, then asks a proud, *How you like me now? Didn't I blow your mind this time, Didn't I?* Nope, typical.

                    MANNY JAMES E
                    HOLIDAY JAMES E   P   ASCAP
                    EMI UNART CATALOG INC   P   BMI
                    UNART UNART

If you shoot an arrow and it goes real/high, hooray for you.

                    PARTICIPANT   P/W   AFFIL
                    HOLIDAY JAMES E   W   ASCAP
                    EMI UNART CATALOG INC
                    UNART UNART

TITLE: HAPPY BIRTHDAY TO MYSELF

                    PARTICIPANT   P/W   AFFIL
                    HOLIDAY JAMES E
                    LEWIS JAMES E   W   BMI
                    EMI UNART CATALOG INC   P   BMI
                    UNART UNART   P   PROCA

Her name is Peaches

HIS NAME IN LIGHTS

He complained of a pleasure with no content. That lasted for three days. Then he disappeared. We smear his echo across our hope/no fear. *I'm dealing with fame as a phobia and a blood type. I'm dealing with the myth that I'm an angel.* Barrel, roll out/Shango cut to soap commercial or rickshaw shield, clearing, slow-motion celebrants—*We did it! We did it!* Reefer helps me focus. And our nerves are never ravens, never coyotes, and weeping waterless tears—And from this moment, *she is the soft master of every scene, the anarchy that silences each category, with her ensemble time.* Smiling like lace on a wing, saturated with truth and moon-flesh, singing doo-wop medleys and glowing like a cash crop. Was your father a singer too? If he didn't beat you, did he at least join you? So subtle but savage, that joy in you/that joy in you is the least of it—the distribution of emphasis across like events until the rebellion is as fast as life and candor is our brightest shield, delivered to the moment where imagination steals memory and he disappears to become one of each. *I'm dealing with fame as a phobia and a blood type. I'm dealing with the myth that I'm an angel.*

The original union of church and state

I found all the images here were bound to business,

I needed it altered

So I spread my legs and drew them in like scissors (more than once)

I cut at the nerve so the through just ruptured of nearer-to god-than-thee
sensation (don't stop there/at
the body's gated jungle resort, but I told the man
It was a nice exercise but it had nothing to do with my life
Take me some place lush and opal, but now!
The leisure aches like newborns-like
Just after birth you begin to wonder if you'll ruin
What you created like you've been (saved)

Fix me, jesus, fix me

Fix me, niggas, fix me

(Almost whispering) (With spring in her heart) *As a robot gets herselves together and we do this, and we get to the middle, where we have remembered our feelings of love, you will tell me, huh?*

WHO CAN I SAY YOU ARE, STARSHINE?

Right View
Right Intention
Right Speech
Right Action
Right Livelihood
Right Effort
Right Mindfulness
Right Concentration
Right Knowledge
Right Liberation
Right Cool
Right Bop
Right Habit
Right Swing
Right Blues
Right Dimension

The Das Racist Blues (Paul Mooney)
The Stability Blues (The Huxtables)
The Unstable Blues (everyone else)

The *Is it a Crime?* **Blues** (Sade)
The Yes Blues (Yes)
The Criminal Minded Blues (Mos Def)
The Extra Name Blues (Yasiin Bey)
The Missing Name Blues (Malcolm X)
The *you don't know what love is* **Blues** (love is war for Miles)
Love isIs a Dangerous Necessity
The *I do* **Blues** (Max Roach/Abbey Lincoln)
The Baby Momma Blues (anonymous)
The Mainstream Blues (Kanye West)
The Third Stream Blues (Sam Rivers)
The Ignant Blues (Tyler Perry)
The Verdict Blues (Errybody)
The Before the Verdict Blues
The Evidence Blues (Monk)
The Missing Black Notes Blues (Rahsaan Roland Kirk)
The *Damn, Son* **Blues**
The *Nah, Son* **Blues** (Dave Chappelle)
The Alchemy Blues (Spike Lee)
The Keep Calm and Hydrate Blues
Nigga, Please (The Nigga Pleasin' Blues)
The Hydrant Game Blues (you already know)

The Style Blues
The Telepathic Blues
The Tell-Tale Heart (Blues)
The Triumph Blues (Barack Obama)
The Numb Blues
The Number Blues
The Number Runner Blues
The Cleverness Blues
The Chronos Blues (Cornel West)
The Yuck! Blues (MF DOOM)
The Button-Up Blues
The Occult Order Blues (Jay-Z)
The Golden Ankh Blues (Badu)
The Needless to Say Blues
The Social Media Blues
The *Treat me right and I'll stay home every day* Blues (Billie Holiday)
The Siiiiike Blues
The Territory Blues (Theaster Gates)
The Blow-Up Blues (Antonioni)
The Come-Up Blues
The What Then Blues
The Total Eclipse of the Heart/ Blues

PARTICIPANT
SHANNON JACKIE
HOLIDAY JAMES F
MYERS RANDY JAMES
EMI UNART CATALOG INC
UNART-UNART

TITLE: I M GONNA HELP HURRY MY BROTHERS HOM

PARTICIPANT
HOLIDAY JAMES E
EMI UNART CATALOG INC
UNART-UNART

TITLE: I M GONNA MOVE TO THE CITY

PARTICIPANT
HOLIDAY JAMES E
EMI UNART CATALOG INC
UNART-UNART

TITLE: I M GONNA USE WHAT I GOT TO GET WHA

PARTICIPANT
HOLIDAY JAMES E
EMI UNART CATALOG INC
UNART-UNART

TITLE: I M NOT ASHAMED

PARTICIPANT
HOLIDAY JAMES E
EMI UNART CATALOG INC
UNART-UNART

TITLE: I M NOT CRYING

AKA: I M NOT CRYING THERE S JUST SMOKE I

The Robot Blues

The Rapper Blues

The Rapper Fetish Blues

The Unbearable Lightness Blues

The Stop Talking About the Blues, Blues

The Nah Blues

The Nodding Blues

The Heroine Blues

The Winning Blues

Melanin on Melanin

The Strata East Blues

The Black Jazz Blues

The Old Black Habit Blues

The Blasphemy Blues

The TV Blues (you be watchin too much)

Redd Foxx's Blues

Sun Ra's Blues

Saturn's Blues

Sarah Vaughn's Blues

Sorrowfully very beautiful, beautiful and blue

Melvin Van Peebles' Blues

Don Cheadle's Blues

Delroy Lindo's Blues

Abbey Lincoln's Blues

Doug Carn's Blues

Jean Carne's Blues

Whitney's Blues

Whitey's Blues

Blue Intensity

If you weren't so convinced, you'd be free

A Red Streak

The Readiness Blues

The *We all Know Whitey's Game* Blues

Goddard's Blues

This *Niggas Are Scared* of the *Revolution* Blues

The *No We Ain't* Blues

Shirley Clarke's Blues

Zora Neale Hurston's Blues

Langston's Blues

Ornette's Blues

True Blues

Famous Blues

My Blues

My Father's Blues

Yours too

Sooner or later

You're gonna want to trade your prayer for a pair of our songs

It won't feel like entertainment. It won't feel like temptation. It'll be when our myth is coming true and undone.

As a robot picks herself apart, to get to the middle, where she has hidden the alchemy of our blues

Right Contradiction
Right devotion
Right hope
Right nobody's fault
Right blame
Right forgiveness
Jazz is beautiful. Jazz is the best.
Right outburst
Right inch-by-inch
Right mile
Right acre
Right mule
Right reprise
Right future

Right all along, all along the watchtower
Right joker
Right thief
Right farmer
Right firmament
Right robin

Right on!

Do you believe any of this?

Right batman

Right sidekick

Right badmind

Right goods

Right services

Right. Play him to the left

Right, *fancy meeting you here*

But we knew all along we could do it

Write the songs they run on and go away walkin'

ACKNOWLEDGMENTS

Take me home with you, there's so much to do, here's a famous blues, are directives that space jazz drummer Tony Williams whispers on his 1970 album, *Turn it Over. Go Find Your Father* is slang for the hero's journey of self-integration that revolutionary/mythologist Joseph Campbell proposes throughout his work. "Do Any Black Children Grow Up Casual?" has appeared in *Poetry Magazine.* Some of the heroes and elective affinities who inspire this text include: Jimmy Hendrix. Jimmy Holiday. Lester Young. Levels and Degrees of Light. James Cahill. Jim Cahill. Mary Helen Cortelette Cahill, Susan Cahill Holiday, Sun Ra, Bill Gun, Chiz Shultz, Raj Advani, Nehprii Amenii, Rebecca Wolff, Theaster Gates, Carrie Mae Weems, Alvin Ailey, Fred Moten, O, Thelonious Monk, James Brown, Billie Holiday, Nina Simone, Amiri Baraka, the wonderful editors at Ricochet Editions, and runners and seekers everywhere. Let us move forward toward our myths.

MORE AT

http://afamousblues.tumblr.com

RICOCHET EDITIONS is an imprint of Gold Line Press, publishing innovative, non-traditional, trans-genre or genre-less works. Both presses are associated with the University of Southern California's PhD in Literature & Creative Writing Program. More information can be found at http://ricocheteditions.com.

COLOPHON

Go Find Your Father / A Famous Blues is typeset in Replica and Joanna MT. Cover image for *Go Find Your Father* is a still from the film *Ganja and Hess,* used with permission. Cover image for *A Famous Blues* is a photograph by Liza Simone Wolff, used with permission. Book design by Diana Arterian and Betsy Medvedovsky